Vintage Baking Recipes

Timeless Tastes From 1800 to 1900

Sign-up Now
and Be Notified of New Books

Website: readbooks.today

Table of Contents

Introduction to "Timeless Tastes: Vintage Baking from 1800-1980"

Every dish tells a story, a narrative woven through time that beckons us to take a glimpse into the past. Baking, a cherished and time-honored tradition, stands as one of the most heartfelt expressions of love, comfort, and creativity across generations. The beauty of baked goods lies not only in their delightful tastes and textures but in their ability to transport us back to different epochs, conjuring memories and evoking deep-rooted emotions. In this cookbook, "Timeless Tastes: Vintage Baking from 1800-1980", we embark on a delectable journey through the annals of baking history, uncovering the hidden gems that graced the tables of our ancestors.

From the dawn of the 19th century to the vibrant 1980s, each decade presented its distinct challenges, innovations, and trends. These eras, shaped by wars, depressions, cultural revolutions, and technological advancements, influenced the way people baked, the ingredients they had access to, and the flavors they craved. The beauty of vintage baking lies in its testament to human resilience and ingenuity — the ability to produce heartwarming, delicious treats even in the most challenging times.

In the 1800s, for instance, baking was a staple in most households. Ingredients were often locally sourced or grown in family gardens, and recipes were passed down verbally from one generation to the next. Bakers relied on the hearth, wood-burning stoves, and their instincts rather than on precise measurements or electric ovens. Simple, robust flavors like the ones in Pound Cake and Sally Lunn Bread captured the essence of this era — where minimalism met delight.

As we traverse into the 20th century, societal shifts and the advent of modern transportation and communication began to change the culinary landscape. The World Wars introduced rationing, leading to innovations like the Wacky Cake, born out of necessity in the absence of eggs, butter, and milk. Yet, despite the challenges, the spirit of baking never waned. In fact, it thrived, giving rise to recipes like the Pineapple Upside-Down Cake and Chocolate Chip Cookies — timeless classics that remain beloved to this day.

The post-war era brought with it an age of experimentation. The 1950s and 60s saw a surge in convenience foods, and baking was not untouched by this trend. Boxed cake mixes and ready-made frostings became household staples. Yet, amidst this convenience revolution, traditional recipes like Red Velvet Cake and Banana Bread persisted, providing a bridge between the old and the new.

As we swing into the 1970s and 80s, a reflection of global influences and a growing interest in gourmet cooking began to emerge. While classics never faded, there was a zest for trying new combinations, textures, and techniques. The Hummingbird Cake, with its tropical flavors, and the rich, multi-layered Opera Cake, are but a couple of examples from this eclectic period.

"Timeless Tastes" isn't just a collection of recipes. It's an ode to the bakers — the grandmothers, mothers, fathers, siblings, and friends who, with flour-dusted hands and passionate hearts, crafted these treats. These recipes are more than just measurements and instructions; they are chronicles of their times, reflections of the societal moods, and most importantly, the embodiment of the love and care of those who baked them.

As you flip through these pages, it is our sincere hope that you not only discover the rich tapestry of baking history but also feel inspired to recreate these vintage wonders in your own kitchen. Whether you're reminiscing about a long-lost family recipe, introducing a classic to a new generation, or simply satiating a craving, this book is your companion, whisking you through time one recipe at a time.

Welcome to "Timeless Tastes." Let's bake history together!

Pound Cake From 1800

Prep: 10 minutes – Cook: 1 hour & 35 minutes – Servings: 8
Calories: 420 – Fat: 21g – Carbs: 49g – Fiber: 2g – Sugar: 31g – Protein: 4g

Enjoy this Vintage Pound Cake as a perfect treat for afternoon tea or any special occasion. Rich buttery and vanilla aroma; evokes a sense of nostalgia for traditional baking. Golden-brown crust with a delicate crispness; visually appealing and reminiscent of classic pound cakes!

Ingredients

- 2 cups granulated sugar
- 1 cup softened unsalted butter (2 sticks), at room temperature
- 4 large eggs, at room temperature
- 1 cup whole milk, at room temperature
- 3 cups all-purpose flour
- 1 teaspoon vanilla extract
- ½ teaspoon salt

Directions

1. Grease and flour a 10-inch tube or Bundt pan and then, preheat your oven to 350 F.
2. In a large mixing bowl, cream together the softened butter and sugar until light and fluffy using an electric mixer.
3. Add the eggs one at a time, beating well after each addition. Scrape down the sides of the bowl as needed.
4. Stir in the vanilla extract.
5. Gradually add the flour and salt to the wet mixture alternately with the milk. Start and end with the flour, mixing until just combined. Be careful not to over mix at this stage.
6. Pour the batter into the prepared pan and spread it evenly.
7. Bake in the preheated oven until a toothpick comes out clean, for 60 to 75 minutes.
8. Let the cake cool in the pan for about 10 minutes and then, transfer it to a wire rack to cool completely.

Sally Lunn Bread From 1805

Prep: 20 minutes – Cook: 3 hours & 35 minutes – Servings: 12
Calories: 220 – Fat: 9g – Carbs: 32g – Fiber: 2g – Sugar: 6g – Protein: 3g

Sally Lunn bread is a traditional English yeast bread that dates back to the 18th century. The exact origins of the bread are debated, but it is believed to have been named after a young French Huguenot immigrant named Solange Luyon, who was known as "Sally Lunn" when she arrived in England. The bread became popular in the city of Bath, England, where it is still celebrated today. Serve warm with butter and jam, making it a delightful addition to a leisurely breakfast or afternoon tea. It can also be used to create delicious sandwiches.

Ingredients

- 4 cups all-purpose flour
- ½ cup softened unsalted butter, at room temperature
- 1 packet active dry yeast (approximately 2 ¼ teaspoon)
- ½ cup granulated sugar
- 3 large eggs, at room temperature
- 1 cup warm milk (around 110 F)
- ½ teaspoon salt

Directions

1. In a small bowl, dissolve the sugar in warm milk. Sprinkle the yeast over the milk mixture and let it sit for about 5-10 minutes until it becomes foamy.
2. In a large mixing bowl, combine the softened butter and flour. Mix until the mixture resembles coarse crumbs.
3. Add the yeast mixture and eggs to the flour mixture. Stir until a soft dough forms.
4. Knead the dough on a lightly floured surface for about 5-7 minutes until it becomes smooth and elastic.
5. Place the dough in a greased bowl, cover it with a clean cloth, and let it rise in a warm place until it doubles in size, for 1 to 1 ½ hours.
6. Preheat your oven to 375 F.
7. Punch down the dough and shape it into a round loaf. Place the dough in a greased 9-inch round cake pan or a similar-sized loaf pan.
8. Cover the dough and let it rise again until it slightly puffs up, for 30 minutes.
9. Bake the Sally Lunn bread in the preheated oven until the top is golden brown and the bread sounds hollow when tapped, for 25-30 minutes.
10. Remove the bread from the pan and let it cool on a wire rack before slicing and serving.

Yorkshire Pudding From 1805

Prep: 20 minutes – Cook: 45 minutes – Servings: 12
Calories: 120 – Fat: 7g – Carbs: 12g – Fiber: 0.3g – Sugar: 2g – Protein 3g

Yorkshire Pudding is a classic British dish with origins dating back to the 18th century. Traditionally, it was served as a side dish alongside a Sunday roast beef dinner. It's made from a simple batter of flour, eggs, and milk, which is baked until puffed and golden brown, creating a hollow center. The key to achieving the classic rise and crispness of Yorkshire Pudding lies in the use of hot beef drippings or oil in the muffin tin. The hot fat causes the batter to puff up dramatically during baking. Yorkshire Pudding can also be enjoyed with other meats and as part of various dishes.

Ingredients

- 1 cup all-purpose flour
- 3 large eggs, at room temperature
- 1 cup whole milk
- 2 tablespoons beef drippings or vegetable oil (traditionally, beef drippings were used for a richer flavor)
- ½ teaspoon salt

Directions

1. Preheat your oven to 450 F. Place a muffin tin or a Yorkshire pudding tin in the oven while it's heating.
2. In a mixing bowl, whisk together the flour, salt, milk, and eggs until you have a smooth, thin batter. It should have a consistency similar to heavy cream.
3. Once the oven is preheated, carefully remove the hot muffin tin or Yorkshire pudding tin. Add about 1/2 to 1 teaspoon of beef drippings or vegetable oil into each well of the tin.
4. Pour the batter into each well, filling them about halfway. The batter should sizzle slightly when it comes into contact with the hot fat.
5. Quickly return the tin to the oven and bake for about 15-20 minutes, or until the puddings are puffed up and golden brown.
6. Serve the Yorkshire Puddings immediately while they are still puffed and crisp. They go wonderfully with roast beef, gravy, and other sides.

Queen Cakes From 1810

Prep: 10 minutes – Cook: 35 minutes – Servings: 12
Calories: 240 – Fat: 12g – Carbs: 31g – Fiber: 1g – Sugar: 14g – Protein: 3g

Queen Cakes are small and individual, making them perfect for tea parties or individual servings. Queen Cakes is a delightful historical treat that dates back to the early 19th century, around the 1810s. These small, individual cakes were popular during the reign of Queen Victoria in England, hence the name "Queen Cakes." They are similar to cupcakes and are known for their light and airy texture, infused with flavors like lemon, currants, and spices. Queen Cakes were traditionally made with currants, but you can also use raisins if desired.

Ingredients

- 1 cup softened unsalted butter, at room temperature (2 sticks)
- 4 large eggs, at room temperature
- ¼ teaspoon ground nutmeg
- 2 cups all-purpose flour
- 1 cup granulated sugar
- ½ cup currants
- 1 teaspoon baking powder
- ¼ teaspoon ground cinnamon
- Zest of 1 lemon
- ¼ cup milk, at room temperature

Directions

1. Line a muffin tin with paper liners or grease the wells and then, preheat your oven to 350 F.
2. In a large mixing bowl, cream together the softened butter and sugar until light and fluffy using an electric mixer.
3. Add the eggs one at a time, beating well after each addition. Scrape down the sides of the bowl as needed.
4. In a separate bowl, whisk together the flour, baking powder, ground nutmeg, and ground cinnamon.
5. Gradually add the dry ingredients to the wet mixture, alternating with the milk. Begin and end with the dry ingredients, mixing until just combined.
6. Stir in the lemon zest and currants (or raisins), distributing them evenly throughout the batter.
7. Spoon the batter into the prepared muffin tin, filling each well about two-thirds full.
8. Bake in the preheated oven until the cakes are lightly golden and a toothpick comes out clean, for 15 to 18 minutes.
9. Remove the Queen Cakes from the oven and let them cool in the tin for a few minutes before transferring them to a wire rack to cool completely.

Tipsy Cake From 1815

Prep: 20 minutes – Cook: 4 hours & 50 minutes – Servings: 10
Calories: 440 – Fat: 30g – Carbs: 49g – Fiber: 1g – Sugar: 34g – Protein: 4g

Tipsy Cake is a classic British dessert that became popular in the 18th and 19th centuries. It is a decadent and indulgent dessert made with sponge cake soaked in a mixture of sherry or other spirits, often layered with custard or cream, and topped with fresh fruit. The dessert is often assembled in a trifle dish or a large glass bowl, showcasing the beautiful layers.

Ingredients

For The Sponge Cake:
- 1 cup granulated sugar
- 4 large eggs, at room temperature
- 1 cup (2 sticks) unsalted butter, softened
- 2 cups all-purpose flour
- 1 teaspoon vanilla extract
- ½ teaspoon salt
- 1 teaspoon baking powder

For The Soaking Syrup:
- ½ cup sherry or other preferred spirit (such as rum or brandy)
- ¼ cup granulated sugar
- ½ cup water

For The Custard:
- 2 cups whole milk
- ½ cup granulated sugar
- 4 large egg yolks
- 1 teaspoon vanilla extract
- ¼ cup cornstarch

For Assembly & Topping:
- Fresh fruit (such as peaches, raspberries, or strawberries) for topping
- 1 cup heavy cream, whipped

Directions

Sponge Cake:
1. Preheat your oven to 350 F. Grease and flour an 8 or 9-inch round cake pan.
2. In a large mixing bowl, cream together the softened butter and sugar until light and fluffy using an electric mixer.
3. Add the eggs one at a time, beating well after each addition. Scrape down the sides of the bowl as needed.
4. In a separate bowl, whisk together the flour, baking powder, and salt.
5. Gradually add the dry ingredients to the wet mixture, mixing until just combined. Stir in the vanilla extract.
6. Pour the batter into the prepared cake pan and spread it evenly.
7. Bake in the preheated oven for about 25-30 minutes or until a toothpick inserted into the center of the cake comes out clean.
8. Let the cake cool in the pan for about 10 minutes, then transfer it to a wire rack to cool completely.

Soaking Syrup:
1. In a small saucepan, combine the sherry (or other spirit), water, and sugar over medium heat. Stir until the sugar dissolves and the mixture is well combined.
2. Remove the syrup from the heat and let it cool to room temperature.

For Custard:
1. In a medium saucepan, heat the milk over medium heat until it starts to steam (do not boil).
2. In a separate bowl, whisk together the egg yolks, sugar, and cornstarch until well combined.
3. Slowly pour the warm milk into the egg yolk mixture while whisking constantly to prevent curdling.
4. Return the mixture to the saucepan and cook over medium heat, stirring constantly, until the custard thickens and coats the back of a spoon.
5. Remove the custard from the heat and stir in the vanilla extract.
6. Let the custard cool to room temperature, then refrigerate it until ready to use.

Assembly:
1. Once the sponge cake has cooled, slice it into 1-inch-thick slices.
2. Arrange a layer of sponge cake slices in the bottom of a trifle dish or a large glass bowl.
3. Drizzle a portion of the soaking syrup over the cake slices, ensuring they are moistened but not soggy.
4. Add a layer of the prepared custard on top of the soaked cake.
5. Repeat the layering process with more cake slices, syrup, and custard until all the ingredients are used, finishing with a layer of custard on top.
6. Cover the dish with plastic wrap and refrigerate for at least 4 hours or overnight to allow the flavors to meld.
7. Before serving, spread the whipped cream over the top layer of custard.
8. Garnish with fresh fruit on top, and you can also sprinkle some grated nutmeg or cinnamon for added flavor.

Doughnuts (early version) From 1820

Prep: 20 minutes – Cook: 40 minutes – Servings: 12
Calories: 160 – Fat: 10g – Carbs: 24g – Fiber: 2g – Sugar: 11g – Protein: 3g

In the early 1820s, doughnuts (also spelled as "donuts") were already a popular treat, but they differed from the modern versions we are familiar with today. Early 19th-century doughnuts were simpler and made with basic ingredients like flour, sugar, eggs, and leavening agents. They were typically fried in fat, such as lard or oil, to achieve a crispy and golden exterior.

Ingredients

- 2 cups all-purpose flour
- ½ cup granulated sugar
- 2 teaspoons baking powder
- ½ cup milk, at room temperature
- 2 large eggs, at room temperature
- ¼ teaspoon ground nutmeg
- 2 tablespoons unsalted butter, melted
- ½ teaspoon salt
- Vegetable oil or lard for frying
- Optional: powdered sugar for dusting

Directions

1. In a large mixing bowl, whisk together the flour, sugar, baking powder, salt, and ground nutmeg.
2. In a separate bowl, whisk the eggs until well beaten. Add the milk and melted butter to the eggs and mix until combined.
3. Pour the wet ingredients into the dry ingredients and stir until just combined. The dough should be soft and slightly sticky.
4. Cover the bowl with a clean cloth and let the dough rest for about 10-15 minutes.
5. In a large, heavy-bottomed pot or deep fryer, heat the vegetable oil or lard to around 350 F.
6. While the oil is heating, lightly flour your work surface and roll out the dough to about 1/2-inch thickness.
7. Use a doughnut cutter or two round cutters of different sizes to cut out doughnut shapes. Alternatively, you can form the dough into small balls for a simpler version.
8. Carefully drop the doughnuts into the hot oil, frying them for about 2-3 minutes on each side or until they turn golden brown.
9. Remove the doughnuts carefully from the oil using a slotted spoon and transfer them to a plate lined with paper towels to drain any excess oil.
10. If desired, while the doughnuts are still warm, you can dust them with powdered sugar for a touch of sweetness.

Scones From 1820

Prep: 20 minutes – Cook: 35 minutes – Servings: 10
Calories: 200 – Fat: 10g – Carbs: 24g – Fiber: 2g – Sugar: 8g – Protein: 4g

Scones have a rich history in British baking and were enjoyed in the early 19th century around 1820. These classic baked goods were originally made with simple ingredients like flour, butter, sugar, and milk, creating a delightful treat to accompany tea or breakfast. Scones could be shaped into rounds and cut into wedges or cut into individual rounds using a cutter.

Ingredients

- ½ cup (1 stick) unsalted butter, cold and cut into small cubes
- 2 cups all-purpose flour
- ½ cup milk
- 1 tablespoon baking powder
- ¼ cup granulated sugar
- ½ cup dried currants, raisins, or chopped dried fruit, optional
- 1 large egg (for egg wash), optional
- ½ teaspoon salt

Directions

1. Preheat your oven to 425 F. Line a baking sheet with parchment paper.
2. In a large mixing bowl, whisk together the flour, sugar, baking powder, and salt.
3. Add the cold, cubed butter to the dry ingredients. Use a pastry blender or your fingers to work the butter into the flour until the mixture resembles coarse crumbs.
4. If you are adding dried fruit to the scones, stir it into the dry mixture.
5. Gradually add the milk to the mixture, stirring until the dough comes together. Be careful not to overmix; the dough should be slightly sticky but manageable.
6. Turn the dough out onto a lightly floured surface. Gently pat or roll the dough to about 1/2 to 3/4 inch thick.
7. Use a round cutter or a sharp knife to cut the dough into scone shapes. Alternatively, you can shape the dough into a round and cut it into wedges.
8. Place the scones on the prepared baking sheet, leaving a little space between each.
9. If desired, whisk the egg and use it to brush the tops of the scones. This will give them a lovely golden color after baking.
10. Bake the scones in the preheated oven until they are lightly golden on top, for 12 to 15 minutes.
11. Remove the scones from the oven and transfer them to a wire rack to cool slightly before serving.

Rice Pudding From 1820

Prep: 20 minutes – Cook: 45 minutes – Servings: 4
Calories: 240 – Fat: 7g – Carbs: 34g – Fiber: 1g – Sugar: 14g – Protein: 4g

Rice pudding has a long history and has been enjoyed in various forms in different cultures around the world for centuries. The early 19th-century version of rice pudding, around 1820, was likely simple and made with basic ingredients available at that time. Ground cinnamon and nutmeg were commonly used to add warm and comforting flavors to the rice pudding.

Ingredients

- ¼ cup granulated sugar
- 2 cups whole milk
- ¼ teaspoon ground cinnamon
- ½ cup short-grain white rice
- ¼ teaspoon ground nutmeg
- ½ teaspoon vanilla extract
- Optional: ¼ cup raisins or currants

Directions

1. In a medium saucepan, rinse the rice under cold water until the water runs clear. Drain the rice.
2. In the same saucepan, combine the rinsed rice, milk, sugar, ground cinnamon, and ground nutmeg.
3. Place the saucepan over medium heat and bring the mixture to a simmer, stirring occasionally to prevent the rice from sticking to the bottom of the pan.
4. Once the mixture reaches a simmer, reduce the heat to low and let the rice cook, uncovered, for about 20-25 minutes or until the rice is tender and the mixture has thickened. Stir occasionally during the cooking process.
5. If using raisins or currants, you can add them to the pudding during the last few minutes of cooking.
6. Once the rice is cooked and the pudding has thickened, remove the saucepan from the heat.
7. Stir in the vanilla extract and adjust the sweetness and spice levels to your taste if needed.
8. Let the rice pudding cool slightly before serving. It can be enjoyed warm, at room temperature, or chilled in the refrigerator.

Shrewsbury Cakes From 1825

Prep: 20 minutes – Cook: 50 minutes – Servings: 24
Calories: 110 – Fat: 6g – Carbs: 12g – Fiber: 1g – Sugar: 7g – Protein: 1g

Shrewsbury Cakes are a delightful historical treat that originated in the town of Shrewsbury, England. They were popular in the 18th and 19th centuries, and their name is associated with the place of origin. These buttery and crumbly cookies were often flavored with lemon and made with simple pantry ingredients, creating a delightful accompaniment to tea or a sweet treat on their own. Sprinkling sugar on top of the cookies before baking added a slight crunch and sweetness to the finished product.

Ingredients

- 1 cup (2 sticks) unsalted butter, softened
- 2 large eggs, at room temperature
- Zest of 1 lemon
- 1 cup granulated sugar
- 3 cups all-purpose flour
- 1 teaspoon baking powder
- A pinch of salt
- Extra sugar, optional, for sprinkling on top

Directions

1. Preheat your oven to 375 F. Line a baking sheet with parchment paper.
2. In a large mixing bowl, cream together the softened butter, sugar, and lemon zest until light and fluffy using an electric mixer.
3. Add the eggs, one at a time, beating well after each addition.
4. In a separate bowl, whisk together the flour, baking powder, and salt.
5. Gradually add dry ingredients t0 mixture, mixing until just combined.
6. Form the dough into a ball, cover it with plastic wrap, and refrigerate it for about 30 minutes to firm up.
7. On a floured surface, roll out the chilled dough to about 1/4 inch thick.
8. Use cookie cutters to cut out shapes from the dough. Traditionally, Shrewsbury Cakes were round, but you can use any shape you like.
9. Place cookies on the baking sheet, leaving a little space between each.
10. Sprinkle sugar on top of cookies for added sweetness and texture.
11. Bake cookies oven 10-12 minutes or until the edges are lightly golden.
12. Remove the baking sheet from the oven and let the cookies cool for a few minutes before transferring them to a wire rack to cool completely.

Welsh Rarebit From 1825

Prep: 2 minutes – Cook: 5 minutes – Servings: 4
Calories: 240 – Fat: 20g – Carbs: 4g – Fiber: 1g – Sugar: 1g – Protein 12g

Welsh Rarebit, also known as Welsh Rabbit, is a classic Welsh dish that dates back to the 18th and 19th centuries, making it a popular meal around 1825. Despite its name, Welsh Rarebit does not actually contain rabbit; instead, it is a savory cheese sauce served over toasted bread. The dish is simple to prepare and has a rich, comforting flavor, making it a popular choice for lunch or a light dinner. Fry or bake some bacon until crispy and crumble it over the Welsh Rarebit for an extra layer of savory flavor and texture. Top the Welsh Rarebit with these onions for a delightful contrast to the cheesy sauce.

Ingredients

- 1 tablespoon all-purpose flour
- 2 cups sharp cheddar cheese, grated
- 1 tablespoon unsalted butter
- ¼ cup beer (traditional choice) or milk
- 1 teaspoon Dijon mustard
- Salt and black pepper to taste
- ½ teaspoon Worcestershire sauce
- 4-6 slices of bread, toasted
- A pinch of cayenne pepper (optional)

Directions

1. In a saucepan over medium heat, melt the butter.
2. Add the flour to the melted butter and whisk together to form a roux. Cook the roux for about a minute, stirring constantly.
3. Gradually add the beer (or milk) to the roux, whisking continuously to create a smooth mixture. The beer will give the dish a traditional flavor, but milk can be used as a non-alcoholic alternative.
4. Stir in the Dijon mustard, Worcestershire sauce, and cayenne pepper (if using). These ingredients add depth and a bit of spiciness to the sauce.
5. Reduce the heat to low, and slowly add the grated cheddar cheese to the sauce, stirring constantly until the cheese is fully melted and the sauce becomes smooth and creamy. Season the sauce with salt and black pepper to taste.
6. Remove the cheese sauce from the heat.
7. Toast the slices of bread until they are lightly browned and crispy.
8. Pour the cheese sauce generously over the toasted bread slices, covering them completely.
9. Optionally, you can place the Welsh Rarebit under a broiler for a minute or two to lightly brown the top and add an appealing crust.

Soft Molasses Cookies From 1830

Prep: 2 minutes – Cook: 1 hour & 10 minutes – Servings: 36
Calories: 80 – Fat: 6g – Carbs: 11g – Fiber: 1g – Sugar: 4g – Protein: 1g

Soft molasses cookies are a delicious and nostalgic treat that has been enjoyed for generations. In the 1830s, these cookies would have been made with simple ingredients commonly available at that time, such as molasses, spices, and basic baking staples. The cookies are soft, chewy, and packed with warm and comforting flavors. Add the zest of one orange to the cookie dough for a bright and citrusy flavor that complements the warm spices. Fold in dried cranberries to the dough for a festive touch and a burst of tartness.

Ingredients

- 1 cup (2 sticks) unsalted butter, softened
- ½ cup molasses (dark or light, according to preference)
- 1 cup granulated sugar
- 2 large eggs, at room temperature
- 1 teaspoon baking soda
- 4 cups all-purpose flour
- 1 teaspoon ground ginger
- ½ teaspoon ground cloves
- 1 teaspoon ground cinnamon
- ½ teaspoon salt
- Granulated sugar (for rolling)

Directions

1. Preheat your oven to 350 F. Line a baking sheet with parchment paper.
2. In a large mixing bowl, cream together the softened butter and granulated sugar until light and fluffy using an electric mixer.
3. Add the molasses to the creamed mixture and mix until well combined.
4. Beat in the eggs, one at a time, until fully incorporated.
5. In a separate bowl, whisk together the flour, baking soda, salt, ground ginger, ground cinnamon, and ground cloves.
6. Gradually add the dry ingredients to the wet mixture, mixing until just combined. Be careful not to overmix the dough.
7. Cover the bowl with plastic wrap and refrigerate the cookie dough for about 30 minutes to an hour. Chilling the dough will make it easier to handle.
8. While the dough is chilling, pour some granulated sugar into a small bowl for rolling the cookie dough.
9. After chilling, scoop out tablespoon-sized portions of dough and roll them into balls using your hands.
10. Roll each dough ball in the granulated sugar until coated all over.
11. Place the sugar-coated dough balls on the prepared baking sheet, leaving enough space between them to allow for spreading during baking.
12. Bake the cookies in the preheated oven for about 10-12 minutes or until they are set and have cracked tops. Remove the baking sheet from the oven and let the cookies cool on the sheet for a few minutes before transferring them to a wire rack to cool completely.

Eccles Cakes From 1830

Prep: 20 minutes – Cook: 55 minutes – Servings: 12
Calories: 200 – Fat 14g – Carbs: 24g – Fiber: 1g – Sugar: 10g – Protein: 3g

Eccles cakes are a classic British pastry that originated in the town of Eccles, England, and were enjoyed during the 19th century, making them a popular treat around 1830. These small, round cakes are filled with a mixture of currants, sugar, and butter, wrapped in flaky pastry, and baked to golden perfection. They are often served as a delightful accompaniment to tea or enjoyed as a sweet snack.

Ingredients

For The Pastry:

- 2 cups all-purpose flour
- ¼ cup granulated sugar
- 1 cup unsalted butter, cold and cut into small cubes
- Ice-cold water, as needed

For The Filling:

- ¼ cup unsalted butter, softened
- 1 cup currants
- ¼ cup brown sugar
- Zest of 1 lemon (optional)
- ½ teaspoon ground cinnamon

Directions

For Pastry:

1. In a large mixing bowl, combine the flour and cold butter cubes. Use your fingertips to rub the butter into the flour until the mixture resembles breadcrumbs.
2. Stir in the granulated sugar.
3. Gradually add ice-cold water, a tablespoon at a time, and mix until the dough comes together. Be careful not to overwork the dough. It should be slightly sticky but manageable.
4. Shape the dough into a ball, cover it with plastic wrap, and refrigerate for at least 30 minutes to chill.

For Filling:

1. In a separate bowl, mix together the currants, softened butter, brown sugar, ground cinnamon, and lemon zest (if using). The mixture should be well combined and slightly moist.

Assembling the Eccles Cakes:

1. Preheat your oven to 375 F.
2. On a lightly floured surface, roll out the chilled pastry dough to a thickness of about 1/8 inch.
3. Using a round cutter or a glass, cut the dough into circles, approximately 4-5 inches in diameter.
4. Place a spoonful of the currant filling in the center of each circle.
5. Fold the pastry over the filling to form a half-moon shape. Seal the edges by pressing them together with your fingers or the tines of a fork.

Baking the Eccles Cakes:

1. Place the filled cakes on a baking sheet lined with parchment paper.
2. Use a sharp knife to make two small slits on the top of each cake to allow steam to escape during baking.
3. Bake the Eccles Cakes in the preheated oven for about 15-20 minutes or until they are golden brown, and the pastry is crisp.

Serving:

1. Remove the Eccles Cakes from the oven and let them cool on a wire rack.
2. Serve the cakes warm or at room temperature. They are best enjoyed on the day of baking.

Lamingtons From 1830

Prep: 20 minutes – Cook: 50 minutes – Servings: 16
Calories: 240 – Fat: 14g – Carbs: 24g – Fiber: 2g – Sugar: 17g – Protein 2g

Lamingtons are squares of sponge cake coated in a layer of chocolate icing and then rolled in desiccated coconut. They are a popular sweet treat in Australia and are often served at afternoon tea or special occasions. While the traditional Lamingtons are coated in chocolate icing and desiccated coconut, you can get creative and add different fillings or coatings, such as jam or whipped cream.

Ingredients

For The Sponge Cake:
- 1 cup granulated sugar
- 4 large eggs, at room temperature
- ½ cup unsalted butter, melted and cooled
- 2 cups all-purpose flour
- ½ cup milk
- 2 teaspoons baking powder
- 1 teaspoon vanilla extract
- ¼ teaspoon salt

For The Chocolate Icing:
- ¼ cup cocoa powder, unsweetened
- 2 cups confectioners' sugar (powdered sugar)
- ½ cup milk
- 2 tablespoons unsalted butter

For Coating:
- 2 cups coconut, desiccated

Directions

Sponge Cake:

1. Preheat your oven to 350 F. Grease and line a square baking pan with parchment paper.
2. In a large mixing bowl, whisk together the eggs and granulated sugar until light and fluffy.
3. In a separate bowl, sift together the flour, baking powder, and salt.
4. Gradually add the dry ingredients to the egg mixture, alternating with the melted butter and milk. Mix until the batter is smooth and well combined.
5. Stir in the vanilla extract.
6. Pour the batter into the prepared baking pan and smooth the top.
7. Bake in the preheated oven for about 25-30 minutes or until a toothpick inserted into the center comes out clean.
8. Remove the cake from the oven and let it cool completely in the pan.

Chocolate Icing:

1. In a medium saucepan, whisk together the powdered sugar and cocoa powder.
2. Add the milk and butter to the saucepan.
3. Place the saucepan over low heat and stir continuously until the mixture is smooth and well combined. Do not let it come to a boil.

Assembling Lamingtons:

1. Once the cake has cooled, remove it from the pan and cut it into squares of your desired size.
2. Place the desiccated coconut in a shallow dish.
3. Dip each cake square into the warm chocolate icing, making sure it is completely coated.
4. Immediately roll the chocolate-coated cake square in the desiccated coconut, pressing gently to adhere the coconut to the icing.
5. Place the coated Lamingtons on a wire rack to set. Repeat the process with the remaining cake squares.

Serving:

1. Once the icing has set, your Lamingtons are ready to be served.
2. Lamingtons are best enjoyed on the day they are made, but they can be stored in an airtight container for a couple of days.

Gingerbread Men From 1835

Prep: 20 minutes – Cook: 2 hours & 45 minutes – Servings: 24
Calories: 120 – Fat: 4g – Carbs: 17g – Fiber: 1g – Sugar: 17g – Protein: 2g

Gingerbread Men are iconic and timeless cookies that have been enjoyed for centuries, making them a popular treat around 1835. These cookies are flavored with warm spices like ginger, cinnamon, and cloves, which give them a distinctive and comforting flavor. They are often shaped into cute little gingerbread men figures and decorated with icing, candies, or raisins. Gingerbread men cookie cutters are traditional, but you can use other shapes or sizes if desired.

Ingredients

- 3 cups all-purpose flour
- 1 teaspoon baking soda
- ½ cup unsalted butter, softened
- 1 tablespoon ground ginger
- ½ teaspoon ground cloves
- 1 tablespoon ground cinnamon
- ½ cup granulated sugar
- 1 large egg, at room temperature
- ½ cup molasses (dark or light, according to preference)
- 1 teaspoon vanilla extract
- ¼ teaspoon salt

Directions

1. In a medium bowl, whisk together the flour, baking soda, salt, ground ginger, ground cinnamon, and ground cloves. Set aside.
2. In a large mixing bowl, cream together the softened butter and granulated sugar until light and fluffy using an electric mixer.

Molasses and Egg:

1. Add the molasses to the creamed butter mixture and mix until well combined.
2. Beat in the egg and vanilla extract until the mixture is smooth and uniform.
3. Gradually add the dry ingredients to the wet mixture, mixing until just combined. Be careful not to overmix the dough.
4. Divide the dough into two equal portions and form each portion into a flat disk shape.
5. Wrap the dough disks with plastic wrap and refrigerate them for at least 1-2 hours or until firm. Chilling the dough will make it easier to roll and cut the cookies.
6. Preheat your oven to 350 F. Line a baking sheet with parchment paper.

Rolling and Cutting:

1. On a lightly floured surface, roll out one chilled dough disk to a thickness of about 1/4 inch.
2. Use gingerbread men cookie cutters to cut out shapes from the rolled dough and place them on the prepared baking sheet, leaving a little space between each cookie.

Baking:

1. Bake the gingerbread men in the preheated oven for about 8-10 minutes or until the edges are lightly browned.
2. Remove the baking sheet from the oven and let the cookies cool on the sheet for a few minutes before transferring them to a wire rack to cool completely.

Decoration:

1. Once the gingerbread men have cooled, you can decorate them with icing, candies, raisins, or other edible decorations of your choice. Use your creativity to give these gingerbread men their own unique personalities!

Almond Macaroons From 1840

Prep: 2 minutes – Cook: 45 minutes – Servings: 20
Calories: 90 – Fat: 6g – Carbs: 9g – Fiber: 1g – Sugar: 6g – Protein: 2g

Almond macaroons are delightful and gluten-free cookies made primarily with almond meal, egg whites, and sugar. These cookies have a chewy texture and a sweet almond flavor, making them a delicious treat. Macaroons were already well-established by the 1840s, and almond macaroons were among the popular variations.

Ingredients

- 2 cups almond meal (ground almonds)
- 1 ¼ cups powdered sugar
- 2 large egg whites, at room temperature
- ¼ teaspoon almond extract
- A pinch of salt
- Whole almonds for decoration (optional)

Directions

1. Preheat your oven to 325 F. Line a baking sheet with parchment paper.
2. In a mixing bowl, combine the almond meal and powdered sugar. Mix well to ensure there are no lumps.
3. In a separate clean bowl, beat the egg whites with a pinch of salt until soft peaks form.
4. Add the almond extract to the beaten egg whites and gently fold it in.
5. Gradually add the dry almond mixture to the beaten egg whites, folding gently until fully combined. The batter should be thick and sticky.
6. If you prefer uniform macaroons, you can use a piping bag fitted with a round tip to pipe small rounds of the batter onto the prepared baking sheet. Leave space between the cookies as they will spread slightly during baking.
7. Alternatively, you can use a spoon to drop small dollops of the batter onto the baking sheet.
8. Optionally, you can place a whole almond on top of each macaroon before baking for added decoration and flavor.
9. Bake the almond macaroons in the preheated oven for about 12-15 minutes or until the edges are golden brown. The centers should remain slightly soft.
10. Remove the baking sheet from the oven and let the macaroons cool on the sheet for a few minutes before transferring them to a wire rack to cool completely.

Apple Charlotte From 1840

Prep: 2 minutes – Cook: 55 minutes – Servings: 6
Calories: 240 – Fat: 14g – Carbs: 40g – Fiber: 2g – Sugar: 24g – Protein: 2g

Apple Charlotte is a classic English dessert that has been enjoyed for centuries, making it a popular treat around 1840. It is a comforting and delicious dessert made with layers of sliced apples and buttered bread, often flavored with sugar, spices, and sometimes lemon zest. The dessert is then baked until the apples are tender, and the bread becomes golden and crispy. Apple Charlotte can be enjoyed on its own or served with a dollop of whipped cream or custard for a more indulgent treat.

Ingredients

- 6-8 medium-sized apples (such as Granny Smith or Bramley), peeled, cored, and thinly sliced
- 1 teaspoon ground cinnamon
- Zest of 1 lemon (optional)
- 6-8 slices of white bread, crusts removed
- Additional butter for greasing the baking dish
- ½ cup unsalted butter, softened
- Whipped cream or custard for serving (optional)
- ½ cup granulated sugar (adjust according to the sweetness of the apples)

Directions

1. Preheat your oven to 375 F. Grease a baking dish (such as a round or rectangular baking dish) with butter.
2. In a bowl, toss the thinly sliced apples with granulated sugar, ground cinnamon, and lemon zest (if using). Make sure the apples are evenly coated with the sugar and spices.
3. Butter each slice of bread on one side, covering it completely with softened butter.
4. Line the bottom and sides of the greased baking dish with the buttered bread slices, buttered side facing out. Slightly overlap the slices to create a continuous layer.
5. Spoon half of the apple mixture into the bread-lined baking dish, spreading it evenly to cover the bread layer.
6. Add another layer of buttered bread slices on top of the apples, again making sure to overlap the slices.
7. Add the remaining apple mixture on top of the second bread layer.
8. Finish with a final layer of buttered bread slices on top of the apples.
9. Gently press down on the layered Apple Charlotte to compress the layers slightly.
10. Cover the baking dish with aluminum foil and bake in the preheated oven for about 30-35 minutes or until the apples are tender.
11. Remove the foil and bake for an additional 10-15 minutes or until the top of the Apple Charlotte is golden and slightly crispy.
12. Remove the Apple Charlotte from the oven and let it cool for a few minutes before serving. Serve warm as is or with a dollop of whipped cream or custard, if desired.

Seed Cake From 1840

Prep: 20 minutes – Cook: 1 hour & 20 minutes – Servings: 10
Calories: 340 – Fat: 19g – Carbs: 34g – Fiber: 2g – Sugar: 20 – Protein: 4g

Seed Cake is a traditional British cake that has been enjoyed for centuries, and it was a popular treat around 1840. It is a delightful and aromatic cake flavored with caraway seeds, which give it a unique and distinct taste. Seed Cake is often served with tea or as a sweet treat for special occasions. The addition of lemon zest is optional but can provide a hint of citrus aroma that complements the caraway seeds.

Ingredients

- 1 ¾ cups all-purpose flour
- 1 cup unsalted butter, softened
- 1 ½ teaspoons baking powder
- 1 cup granulated sugar
- 4 large eggs, at room temperature
- 1 teaspoon vanilla extract
- ¼ cup milk
- 1 tablespoon caraway seeds
- Zest of 1 lemon (optional)
- ¼ teaspoon salt

Directions

1. Preheat your oven to 350 F. Grease and line a loaf pan with parchment paper.
2. In a medium bowl, whisk together the all-purpose flour, baking powder, and salt. Set aside.
3. In a large mixing bowl, cream together the softened butter and granulated sugar until light and fluffy using an electric mixer.
4. Add the eggs one at a time, beating well after each addition.
5. Stir in the vanilla extract.
6. Fold in the caraway seeds and lemon zest (if using) into the butter mixture.
7. Gradually add the dry ingredients to the wet mixture, alternating with the milk. Begin and end with the dry ingredients.
8. Mix until just combined. Do not overmix.
9. Pour the cake batter into the prepared loaf pan and spread it evenly.
10. Bake in the preheated oven for about 40-50 minutes or until a toothpick inserted into the center comes out clean.
11. Remove the Seed Cake from the oven and let it cool in the pan for about 10 minutes.
12. Transfer the cake to a wire rack to cool completely.

Washington Cake From 1845

Prep: 2 minutes – Cook: 1 hour & 25 minutes – Servings: 12
Calories: 340 – Fat: 16g – Carbs: 40g – Fiber: 2g – Sugar: 22g – Protein: 4g

Washington Cake is a historical American dessert that dates back to the 19th century, around 1845. It is named after George Washington, the first President of the United States, and is believed to be one of his favorite cakes. Washington Cake is a type of pound cake made with simple ingredients such as flour, butter, sugar, eggs, and flavorings. It is traditionally served with a light glaze or icing. Washington Cake is delightful on its own or served with fresh berries or a scoop of ice cream.

Ingredients

- 5 large eggs, at room temperature
- 1 cup (2 sticks) unsalted butter, softened
- 2 cups granulated sugar
- 1 teaspoon vanilla extract
- 3 cups all-purpose flour
- 1 teaspoon baking powder
- ¼ teaspoon salt
- 1 cup milk
- Zest of 1 lemon (optional, for a citrus flavor)

For The Glaze:
- 2-3 tablespoons milk or lemon juice
- 1 cup powdered sugar
- ½ teaspoon vanilla extract

Directions

1. Preheat your oven to 350 F. Grease and flour a Bundt pan or tube pan.
2. In a large mixing bowl, cream together the softened butter and granulated sugar until light and fluffy using an electric mixer.
3. Add the eggs one at a time, beating well after each addition.
4. Stir in the vanilla extract and lemon zest (if using).
5. In a separate bowl, whisk together the all-purpose flour, baking powder, and salt.
6. Gradually add the dry ingredients to the wet mixture, alternating with the milk. Begin and end with the dry ingredients.
7. Mix until just combined. Do not overmix.
8. Pour the cake batter into the prepared Bundt pan or tube pan and spread it evenly.
9. Bake in the preheated oven for about 50-60 minutes or until a toothpick inserted into the center comes out clean.
10. Remove the cake from the oven and let it cool in the pan for about 10 minutes.
11. Transfer the cake to a wire rack to cool completely.

For Glaze:
1. In a small bowl, whisk together the powdered sugar, milk or lemon juice, and vanilla extract until smooth.
2. Once the cake has cooled, drizzle the glaze over the top of the cake, allowing it to drip down the sides.
3. Let the glaze set for a few minutes before serving the Washington Cake.

Plum Pudding From 1845

Prep: 20 minutes – Cook: 5 hours & 30 minutes – Servings: 10
Calories: 400 – Fat: 20g – Carbs: 49g – Fiber: 3g – Sugar: 34g – Protein: 7g

Plum Pudding, also known as Christmas Pudding or Plum Duff, is a traditional British dessert that has been enjoyed for centuries, and it was a popular treat around the mid-19th century, including 1845. Despite its name, Plum Pudding doesn't actually contain plums; historically, "plum" referred to any dried fruit. Plum Pudding is typically made with a variety of dried fruits, suet (beef or vegetable fat), breadcrumbs, flour, eggs, sugar, and spices. It is traditionally steamed, giving it a dense and moist texture, and is often served during the Christmas season.

Ingredients

- 1 cup suet (vegetable or beef suet), grated or finely chopped
- ½ cup almonds or other nuts, chopped
- 1 cup mixed dried fruits (such as currants, raisins, sultanas, candied peel)
- ½ teaspoon ground nutmeg
- 1 cup all-purpose flour
- ¼ teaspoon ground cloves
- 1 cup fresh breadcrumbs
- ¼ teaspoon ground ginger
- A pinch of salt
- 1 cup brown sugar
- ½ cup milk
- 3 large eggs, beaten
- 1 teaspoon ground cinnamon
- ¼ cup brandy or dark rum (optional, for soaking the pudding)
- Vegetable oil or butter, for greasing

For Serving:
- Custard or brandy butter (traditional accompaniments)
- Brandy or dark rum (for flambéing, optional)

Directions

1. Grease a heatproof pudding basin or mold (about 1.5-quart capacity) with butter or vegetable oil.
2. In a large mixing bowl, combine the suet, all-purpose flour, breadcrumbs, brown sugar, mixed dried fruits, chopped nuts (if using), ground cinnamon, ground nutmeg, ground cloves, ground ginger, and a pinch of salt. Mix well until all ingredients are evenly distributed.
3. In a separate bowl, whisk together the milk and beaten eggs.
4. Gradually pour the milk and egg mixture into the dry ingredients, stirring as you go, until a thick and moist batter forms. The mixture should be evenly combined, but not too wet.
5. Transfer the pudding batter into the greased pudding basin or mold.
6. Cover the basin with a double layer of parchment paper or aluminum foil, securing it with a string or a lid.
7. Place the pudding basin in a large saucepan or steamer with enough water to come about halfway up the sides of the basin.
8. Cover the saucepan with a lid and steam the pudding over low to medium heat for about 4 to 5 hours. Check the water level periodically and top up if needed.
9. Once the pudding is steamed, remove it from the heat and let it cool slightly in the basin before turning it out onto a serving plate.
10. If desired, you can drizzle the brandy or dark rum over the hot pudding and allow it to soak in. This step is optional but adds extra flavor.
11. Serve the Plum Pudding warm with traditional accompaniments such as custard or brandy butter.
12. If you want to add a festive touch, you can flambé the pudding by heating some brandy or dark rum, pouring it over the pudding, and lighting it with a long match (use caution when doing this).

African Cake (a type of fruitcake) From 1850

Prep: 20 minutes – Cook: 2 hours & 35 minutes – Servings: 12
Calories: 340 – Fat: 20g – Carbs: 49g – Fiber: 2g – Sugar: 34g – Protein: 4g

African Cake, also known as Jamaican Fruit Cake or Black Cake, is a rich and flavorful type of fruitcake that has its origins in the Caribbean, particularly Jamaica. It is traditionally enjoyed during special occasions, such as Christmas and weddings. The cake is called "Black Cake" due to its dark color, which comes from the use of dark molasses, brown sugar, and the addition of rum or wine-soaked dried fruits. This recipe includes the use of rum-soaked fruits. You can adjust the amount of alcohol or use fruit juice if you prefer a non-alcoholic version.

Ingredients

For Rum-Soaked Fruits:
- 1 cup dark rum (or wine, fruit juice)
- 1 cup mixed dried fruits (prunes, currants, raisins, cherries, etc.)

For Cake Batter:
- 1 teaspoon baking powder
- ½ teaspoon baking soda
- 1 cup unsalted butter, softened
- ¼ teaspoon ground allspice
- 1 cup brown sugar
- 2 cups all-purpose flour
- 4 large eggs, at room temperature
- ½ cup dark molasses
- 1 teaspoon vanilla extract
- ½ teaspoon ground nutmeg
- 1 teaspoon ground cinnamon
- ½ cup chopped nuts (such as almonds or walnuts, optional)
- Zest of 1 orange or lemon (optional)
- ¼ teaspoon salt

Directions

1. In a bowl, combine the mixed dried fruits with dark rum (or wine, fruit juice).
2. Cover the bowl and let the fruits soak for at least 24 hours, preferably longer, to allow the flavors to develop.
3. Preheat your oven to 325 F. Grease and line a round or square cake pan with parchment paper.
4. In a medium bowl, whisk together the all-purpose flour, baking powder, baking soda, and salt. Set aside.
5. In a large mixing bowl, cream together the softened butter and brown sugar until light and fluffy using an electric mixer.
6. Add the eggs one at a time, beating well after each addition.
7. Stir in the dark molasses and vanilla extract.
8. Mix in the ground cinnamon, ground nutmeg, ground allspice, and zest of one orange or lemon (if using).
9. Gradually add the dry ingredients to the wet mixture, mixing until just combined.
10. Stir in the rum-soaked fruits (and any remaining liquid) and chopped nuts (if using).
11. Pour the cake batter into the prepared cake pan and spread it evenly.
12. Bake in the preheated oven for about 1.5 to 2 hours or until a toothpick inserted into the center comes out clean.
13. Remove the cake from the oven and let it cool in the pan for about 10 minutes.
14. Transfer the cake to a wire rack to cool completely.

Chess Pie From 1850

Prep: 10 minutes – Cook: 1 hour & 15 minutes – Servings: 10
Calories: 300 – Fat: 14g – Carbs: 34g – Fiber: 2g – Sugar: 24g – Protein: 4g

Chess Pie is a classic and delicious dessert that has its origins in the southern United States, and it was popular around the mid-19th century, including 1850. It is a simple pie made with pantry staples like eggs, sugar, butter, and a small amount of flour, resulting in a sweet and custardy filling. The name "Chess Pie" has various explanations for its origin, but none are definitive.

Ingredients

- 1 unbaked pie crust (store-bought or homemade)
- ½ cup unsalted butter, melted and cooled slightly
- 1 tablespoon all-purpose flour
- 1 cup granulated sugar
- 4 large eggs, at room temperature
- 1 tablespoon cornmeal (optional, for added texture)
- ¼ cup whole milk
- 1 tablespoon white vinegar or apple cider vinegar
- A pinch of salt
- 1 teaspoon vanilla extract

Directions

1. Preheat your oven to 350 F. Place the unbaked pie crust in a 9-inch pie dish. You can crimp or flute the edges if desired.
2. In a large mixing bowl, whisk together the granulated sugar and melted butter until well combined.
3. Add the eggs, one at a time, to the sugar-butter mixture, whisking well after each addition.
4. Stir in the whole milk.
5. If using cornmeal, whisk in the tablespoon of cornmeal for added texture. Then, add the all-purpose flour and whisk until smooth.
6. Mix in the vanilla extract and the white vinegar (or apple cider vinegar).
7. Add a pinch of salt to enhance the flavors.
8. Pour the Chess Pie filling into the unbaked pie crust, spreading it evenly.
9. Bake the pie in the preheated oven for about 40 to 45 minutes or until the filling is set. It should have a slight jiggle in the center, but not be too liquidy.
10. Remove the Chess Pie from the oven and let it cool completely on a wire rack.
11. Once the pie is cooled, it is ready to be served. You can serve it at room temperature or chilled, depending on your preference.

Butter Tart From 1850

Prep: 20 minutes – Cook: 55 minutes – Servings: 12
Calories: 340 – Fat: 20g – Carbs: 40g – Fiber: 2g – Sugar: 24g – Protein: 3g

Butter Tart is a classic and delectable Canadian pastry that has been enjoyed for generations. While the exact origins of Butter Tarts are not well-documented, they have been a beloved treat in Canada since the 1800s. The tart consists of a flaky pastry shell filled with a mixture of butter, sugar, and eggs, often with the addition of syrup or other ingredients like raisins or nuts.

Ingredients

For Pastry:

- ½ cup unsalted butter, chilled and cut into small pieces
- 1 ½ cups all-purpose flour
- ¼ cup granulated sugar
- 3-4 tablespoons ice-cold water
- A pinch of salt

For Filling:

- ½ cup unsalted butter, melted
- 1 cup packed brown sugar
- ¼ cup maple syrup or corn syrup
- 2 large eggs
- ¼ cup chopped nuts (such as walnuts or pecans, optional)
- 1 teaspoon vanilla extract
- ¼ cup raisins (optional)

Directions

1. Preheat your oven to 375 F. Grease a muffin tin or tart pans.
2. In a mixing bowl, combine the all-purpose flour, granulated sugar, and a pinch of salt.
3. Add the chilled, diced butter to the dry ingredients. Use a pastry cutter or your fingers to cut the butter into the flour mixture until it resembles coarse crumbs.
4. Gradually add ice-cold water, one tablespoon at a time, and mix until the dough comes together. Be careful not to overwork the dough.
5. Form the dough into a ball, wrap it in plastic wrap, and refrigerate for at least 30 minutes.
6. In a mixing bowl, whisk together the melted butter, packed brown sugar, eggs, vanilla extract, and maple syrup (or corn syrup) until smooth and well combined.
7. If using raisins or chopped nuts, add them to the filling mixture and stir until evenly distributed.
8. On a lightly floured surface, roll out the chilled pastry dough to about 1/8-inch thickness.
9. Use a round cookie cutter or a glass to cut out circles slightly larger than the size of the muffin tin or tart pans. Gently press each circle into the cavities to form the tart shells.
10. Spoon the prepared filling into each pastry shell, filling them about two-thirds full.
11. Bake the Butter Tarts in the preheated oven for about 15-20 minutes or until the pastry is golden and the filling is set with a slight jiggle in the center.
12. Remove the Butter Tarts from the oven and let them cool in the muffin tin or tart pans for a few minutes before transferring them to a wire rack to cool completely.

Peach Cobbler From 1850

Prep: 20 minutes – Cook: 55 minutes – Servings: 10
Calories: 240 – Fat: 9g – Carbs: 34g – Fiber: 1g – Sugar: 16g – Protein: 3g

Peach Cobbler is a classic and beloved American dessert that has been enjoyed for centuries. Although the exact origin of Peach Cobbler is not well-documented, fruit cobblers like this one have been enjoyed by early American settlers. A Peach Cobbler typically consists of sweetened, spiced peaches topped with a buttery biscuit or cake-like topping and baked to golden perfection.

Ingredients

For Peach Filling:
- ¼ teaspoon ground nutmeg
- 6 cups fresh or canned peaches, peeled and sliced (approximately 6-8 medium peaches)
- ½ teaspoon ground cinnamon
- 1 tablespoon all-purpose flour
- ½ teaspoon vanilla extract (optional, for added flavor)
- 1 tablespoon lemon juice (optional, for a hint of tartness)
- ½ to ¾ cup granulated sugar (adjust based on the sweetness of the peaches)

For Cobbler Topping:
- 1 cup all-purpose flour
- ¼ cup whole milk
- 2 tablespoons granulated sugar
- ¼ cup unsalted butter, chilled and cut into small pieces
- 1 ½ teaspoons baking powder
- 1 large egg, lightly beaten
- ¼ teaspoon salt

Directions

For Peach Filling:

1. Preheat your oven to 375 F. Grease a 9x13-inch baking dish or a similar-sized deep dish.
2. In a large mixing bowl, combine the sliced peaches, granulated sugar, all-purpose flour, ground cinnamon, ground nutmeg, lemon juice (if using), and vanilla extract (if using). Toss the mixture gently until the peaches are well coated.

Assembling the Cobbler:

1. Transfer the peach filling to the greased baking dish, spreading it evenly.

For Cobbler Topping:

1. In a separate mixing bowl, whisk together the all-purpose flour, granulated sugar, baking powder, and salt.
2. Add the chilled, diced butter to the dry ingredients. Use a pastry cutter or your fingers to cut the butter into the flour mixture until it resembles coarse crumbs.
3. Gradually add the whole milk and lightly beaten egg to the flour-butter mixture. Stir until a soft and slightly sticky dough forms.
4. Drop spoonfuls of the cobbler dough onto the peach filling, covering it as evenly as possible.

Baking the Peach Cobbler:

1. Bake the Peach Cobbler in the preheated oven for about 30 to 35 minutes or until the cobbler topping is golden and cooked through.
2. Cooling and Serving:
3. Remove the Peach Cobbler from the oven and let it cool slightly before serving. You can enjoy it warm or at room temperature.

Suet Pudding From 1850

Prep: 20 minutes – Cook: 2 hours & 35 minutes – Servings: 6
Calories: 340 – Fat: 23g – Carbs: 40g – Fiber: 2g – Sugar: 24g – Protein: 4g

Suet pudding was a popular and hearty dessert enjoyed in various parts of the world, including the United Kingdom and North America. Suet is the hard, white fat found around the kidneys and loins of animals, often used in traditional British cooking to add richness and flavor to dishes.

Ingredients

For The Pudding:
- 1 cup all-purpose flour
- ½ cup shredded beef suet (or vegetable suet for a vegetarian version)
- ½ cup breadcrumbs
- ½ cup granulated sugar
- 1 teaspoon ground cinnamon
- ½ teaspoon ground nutmeg
- ¼ teaspoon ground cloves
- ½ cup milk
- 1 large egg, beaten
- ½ cup dried fruits (such as raisins, currants, or sultanas)
- ¼ cup chopped candied peel (optional)
- Butter or oil for greasing

For the Sauce (Optional):
- ½ cup unsalted butter
- ½ cup granulated sugar
- ½ cup heavy cream

Directions

For The Pudding:

1. Grease a 1-quart pudding basin or heatproof bowl with butter or oil.
2. Mixing the Dry Ingredients:
3. In a large mixing bowl, combine the all-purpose flour, shredded suet, breadcrumbs, granulated sugar, ground cinnamon, ground nutmeg, and ground cloves. Mix well.
4. In a separate bowl, whisk together the milk and beaten egg.
5. Gradually add the milk-egg mixture to the dry ingredients, stirring to form a smooth and thick batter.
6. Fold in the dried fruits and chopped candied peel (if using) into the batter, ensuring they are evenly distributed.
7. Transfer the pudding batter into the greased pudding basin, pressing it down gently.
8. Cover the pudding basin with a greased piece of parchment paper, and then cover it with aluminum foil, securing it tightly with a string or rubber band.
9. Place the pudding basin in a large pot or saucepan with enough water to reach halfway up the sides of the basin.
10. Bring the water to a gentle simmer, cover the pot with a lid, and steam the pudding for about 2 to 2.5 hours. Check the water level occasionally and top it up if needed.

Serving:

1. Once the pudding is steamed, carefully remove it from the pot and let it cool slightly.
2. Turn out the pudding onto a serving plate.

For the Sauce (Optional):

1. In a saucepan, melt the unsalted butter over medium heat.
2. Stir in the granulated sugar and heavy cream and cook the mixture over medium heat until it thickens slightly to form a rich sauce.

Serving:

1. Pour the sauce over the steamed suet pudding just before serving. The sauce adds extra sweetness and creaminess to the dessert.

Flannel Cakes (early pancakes) From 1855

Prep: 20 minutes – Cook: 45 minutes – Servings: 10
Calories: 130 – Fat: 6g – Carbs: 17g – Fiber: 1g – Sugar: 4g – Protein: 3g

Flannel Cakes, also known as Flapjacks or early pancakes, were a popular breakfast dish. They were made using simple ingredients that were easily available during that time. Flannel Cakes are similar to modern pancakes but may have slight variations in ingredients and preparation. Depending on the region and the cook's preferences, there may have been slight variations in the recipe, such as the addition of spices like cinnamon or nutmeg.

Ingredients

- 1 cup all-purpose flour
- ½ teaspoon baking soda
- 1 large egg
- 2 tablespoons melted butter or lard (or other available fat)
- 1 teaspoon baking powder
- A pinch of salt
- 1 cup buttermilk (or milk, if buttermilk is not available)
- Additional butter or oil for greasing the griddle
- 1 tablespoon granulated sugar

Directions

1. Preheat a griddle or a large flat frying pan over medium heat.
2. In a mixing bowl, whisk together the all-purpose flour, granulated sugar, baking powder, baking soda, and a pinch of salt. In a separate bowl, whisk together the buttermilk (or milk), egg, and melted butter (or lard).
3. Gradually add the wet ingredients to the dry ingredients, stirring until just combined. The batter should have a slightly lumpy consistency. Grease the preheated griddle or frying pan with butter or oil. Pour about 1/4 cup of the batter onto the griddle for each Flannel Cake. Cook until bubbles appear on the surface and the edges look set, which usually takes about 2-3 minutes.
4. Flip the Flannel Cakes and cook for an additional 1-2 minutes on the other side or until golden brown and cooked through. Serve the Flannel Cakes warm with your favorite toppings, such as maple syrup, honey, butter, jam, or fresh fruit.

Boston Cream Pie From 1855

Prep: 20 minutes – Cook: 55 minutes – Servings: 10
Calories: 440 – Fat: 24g – Carbs: 49g – Fiber: 2g – Sugar: 34g – Protein: 6g

The Boston Cream Pie is a classic and iconic American dessert that has a rich history dating back to the mid-19th century. Despite its name, Boston Cream Pie is actually a cake, not a traditional pie. The original version of the Boston Cream Pie was created by French chef M. Sanzian at the Parker House Hotel in Boston, Massachusetts, in 1855. The cake consists of two layers of sponge or butter cake filled with custard and topped with a chocolate glaze.

Ingredients

For Sponge Cake Layers:
- 1 cup all-purpose flour
- 4 large eggs, at room temperature
- 1 cup granulated sugar
- ½ cup whole milk
- 1 teaspoon vanilla extract
- ¼ teaspoon salt
- 1 teaspoon baking powder

For Custard Filling:
- 2 cups whole milk
- ¼ cup cornstarch
- 4 large egg yolks
- 1 teaspoon vanilla extract
- ½ cup granulated sugar

For Chocolate Glaze:
- 1 cup semisweet chocolate chips or chopped chocolate
- ½ cup heavy cream
- 1 tablespoon unsalted butter

Directions

For Sponge Cake Layers:
1. Preheat your oven to 350 F. Grease and flour two 9-inch round cake pans.
2. In a mixing bowl, whisk together the all-purpose flour, baking powder, and salt. Set aside.
3. In a separate large mixing bowl, beat the eggs and granulated sugar together using an electric mixer until pale and fluffy.
4. Mix in the vanilla extract, and then gradually add the whole milk while continuing to mix.
5. Gradually add the dry ingredients to the wet ingredients, mixing until just combined and no lumps remain.

Baking:
1. Divide the batter evenly between the prepared cake pans. Bake in the preheated oven for about 20-25 minutes or until a toothpick inserted into the center comes out clean.
2. Remove the cake layers from the oven and let them cool in the pans for a few minutes before transferring them to a wire rack to cool completely.

For Custard Filling:
1. Heating Milk: In a saucepan, heat the whole milk over medium heat until it begins to steam, but do not let it boil.
2. In a separate bowl, whisk together the egg yolks and granulated sugar until well combined.
3. Gradually whisk the warm milk into the egg yolk mixture, making sure to whisk constantly to avoid curdling.
4. Return the mixture to the saucepan and cook over medium heat, stirring constantly until it thickens and coats the back of a spoon.
5. Remove the custard from the heat and stir in the vanilla extract.
6. Transfer the custard to a bowl and cover the surface with plastic wrap to prevent a skin from forming.
7. Refrigerate the custard until completely cooled.

Assembling the Boston Cream Pie:
1. Filling the Cake:
2. Once the cake layers and custard are completely cooled, place one cake layer on a serving plate.
3. Spread the cooled custard evenly over the top of the first cake layer.

Top Layer:
1. Place the second cake layer on top of the custard, creating a cake sandwich.

For Chocolate Glaze:
1. Heating Cream: In a saucepan, heat the heavy cream over medium heat until it begins to steam, but do not let it boil.
2. Remove the saucepan from the heat and add the semisweet chocolate chips or chopped chocolate and unsalted butter.
3. Stir until the chocolate and butter are fully melted and the glaze is smooth.

Glazing the Cake:
1. Pour the warm chocolate glaze over the top of the assembled Boston Cream Pie, spreading it evenly and allowing it to drip down the sides.
2. Let the Boston Cream Pie cool slightly to set the glaze before serving.

Anzac Biscuits From 1860

Prep: 20 minutes – Cook: 45 minutes – Servings: 18
Calories: 140 – Fat: 6g – Carbs: 14g – Fiber: 1g – Sugar: 7g – Protein: 1g

Anzac Biscuits are a popular and classic Australian sweet treat with a storied history dating back to the 19th century. The name "Anzac" stands for "Australian and New Zealand Army Corps," and these biscuits were originally made and sent by families to soldiers serving during World War I. Anzac Biscuits are known for their simple ingredients and long shelf life, making them ideal for transportation overseas. Golden syrup is a key ingredient in traditional Anzac Biscuits, providing sweetness and flavor. If you don't have golden syrup, you can use corn syrup or honey as a substitute.

Ingredients

- 1 cup all-purpose flour
- ¾ cup granulated sugar
- 1 cup desiccated coconut
- 2 tablespoons golden syrup
- 1 cup rolled oats
- ½ cup unsalted butter
- 1 tablespoon boiling water
- ½ teaspoon baking soda

Directions

1. Preheat your oven to 350 F. Line a baking sheet with parchment paper.
2. In a mixing bowl, combine the all-purpose flour, rolled oats, desiccated coconut, and granulated sugar.
3. In a small saucepan, melt the unsalted butter over low heat.
4. Stir in the golden syrup (or substitute) until well combined.
5. In a separate small bowl, dissolve the baking soda in the boiling water.
6. Add the baking soda mixture to the melted butter and syrup mixture, stirring well.
7. Pour the wet ingredients over the dry ingredients and mix until everything is thoroughly combined.
8. Take spoonfuls of the biscuit mixture and roll them into balls. Place the balls onto the prepared baking sheet, leaving some space between each one.
9. Use the back of a spoon or your fingers to lightly flatten each ball to form a biscuit shape.
10. Bake the Anzac Biscuits in the preheated oven for about 10-12 minutes or until they are golden brown.
11. Remove the biscuits from the oven and let them cool on the baking sheet for a few minutes before transferring them to a wire rack to cool completely.

Spotted Dick From 1860

Prep: 10 minutes – Cook: 3 hours & 25 minutes – Servings: 6
Calories: 240 – Fat: 11g – Carbs: 24g – Fiber: 1g – Sugar: 16g – Protein: 3g

Spotted Dick is a traditional British pudding that dates back to the 19th century, specifically the 1860s. It is a steamed or boiled dessert made with suet, dried fruits, and flour. The name "Spotted Dick" likely comes from the "spotted" appearance of the dried fruits in the pudding and the term "dick," which was a common word for pudding in the past.

Ingredients

- 1 cup all-purpose flour
- ½ cup shredded beef suet (or vegetable suet for a vegetarian version)
- 1 teaspoon baking powder
- ½ cup mixed dried fruits (such as raisins, currants, and sultanas)
- Zest of 1 lemon (optional, for added flavor)
- 1 large egg, beaten
- Butter or oil for greasing
- ½ cup granulated sugar
- Pinch of salt
- ½ cup milk
- Golden syrup or custard, for serving (optional)

Directions

1. Grease a 1-quart pudding basin or heatproof bowl with butter or oil.
2. In a mixing bowl, whisk together the all-purpose flour, shredded suet, granulated sugar, mixed dried fruits, lemon zest (if using), baking powder, and a pinch of salt.
3. In a separate bowl, whisk together the milk and beaten egg.
4. Gradually add the wet ingredients to the dry ingredients, stirring until just combined. The mixture should have a slightly sticky consistency.
5. Transfer the pudding mixture into the greased pudding basin, pressing it down gently.
6. Cover the pudding basin with a greased piece of parchment paper, and then cover it with aluminum foil, securing it tightly with a string or rubber band.
7. To steam the pudding: Place the pudding basin in a large pot or saucepan with enough water to reach halfway up the sides of the basin. Bring the water to a gentle simmer, cover the pot with a lid, and steam the pudding for about 2 to 2.5 hours. Check the water level occasionally and top it up if needed.
8. To boil the pudding: Place the covered pudding basin in a large pot or saucepan. Fill the pot with enough water to reach about halfway up the sides of the basin. Bring the water to a boil, then reduce the heat to a simmer. Cover the pot with a lid and boil the pudding for about 2 to 2.5 hours. Check the water level occasionally and add more boiling water if needed.
9. Once the pudding is cooked, carefully remove it from the pot and let it cool slightly before turning it out onto a serving plate.

Treacle Tart From 1860

Prep: 10 minutes – Cook: 1 hour & 10 minutes – Servings: 10
Calories: 300 – Fat: 14g – Carbs: 39g – Fiber: 2g – Sugar: 20g – Protein: 3g

Treacle Tart is a classic British dessert with a history that dates back to the 19th century, around the 1860s. It is a sweet and comforting tart made with a filling of golden syrup (treacle) and breadcrumbs. Treacle Tart has been a favorite in British cuisine for generations and is still enjoyed today. Add chopped nuts such as almonds, walnuts, or pecans to the treacle filling. The nuts will provide a delightful crunch and nutty flavor to the tart. Increase the amount of ground ginger and ground cinnamon in the filling to enhance the spiced flavor profile of the tart. You can also add a pinch of ground cloves or nutmeg for additional warmth.

Ingredients

For Pastry:

- 1 ¼ cups all-purpose flour
- 1 large egg, beaten
- ½ cup unsalted butter, chilled and diced
- 1-2 tablespoons cold water (as needed)
- ¼ cup granulated sugar

For Filling:

- Zest and juice of 1 lemon
- 1 ½ cups golden syrup (treacle)
- A pinch of ground ginger (optional, for added flavor)
- 1 ½ cups fresh white breadcrumbs (made from day-old white bread)
- A pinch of ground cinnamon (optional, for added flavor)

Directions

For Pastry:
1. Preheat your oven to 375 F. Grease a 9-inch tart tin or pie dish.
2. Mixing the Ingredients:
3. In a mixing bowl, combine the all-purpose flour, diced unsalted butter, and granulated sugar.
4. Rub the butter into the flour mixture using your fingertips until the mixture resembles breadcrumbs.
5. Add the beaten egg to the mixture and mix until the dough starts to come together. If the dough is too dry, add cold water, one tablespoon at a time, until the dough forms a ball.
6. On a lightly floured surface, roll out the pastry to fit the greased tart tin or pie dish.
7. Carefully transfer the rolled-out pastry to the tart tin or pie dish, pressing it gently into the edges and sides.
8. Trim any excess pastry from the edges of the tin or dish. You can crimp the edges for a decorative touch if desired.

For Filling:
1. In a mixing bowl, combine the golden syrup (treacle), fresh white breadcrumbs, lemon zest, lemon juice, ground ginger (if using), and ground cinnamon (if using). Mix until well combined.
2. Pour the treacle filling into the prepared pastry shell, spreading it evenly.

Baking:
1. Bake the Treacle Tart in the preheated oven for about 20-25 minutes or until the filling is set and the pastry is golden brown.
2. Cooling and Serving:
3. Allow the Treacle Tart to cool slightly before serving.

Mince Pie From 1865

Prep: 20 minutes – Cook: 55 minutes – Servings: 10
Calories: 340 – Fat: 16g – Carbs: 40g – Fiber: 2g – Sugar: 24g – Protein: 3g

Mince pie, also known as mincemeat pie, was a popular dessert in the United States and the United Kingdom. Traditional mince pies date back to medieval times and have evolved over the centuries. While the original recipe included meat, such as beef or mutton, the version popular in the 19th century typically omitted meat and focused on dried fruits, spices, and brandy or other spirits. Traditionally, mince pies are often enjoyed during the holiday season, especially during Christmas.

Ingredients

For Mincemeat Filling:
- ½ cup chopped dried apples
- 1 cup raisins
- ½ cup candied peel, chopped
- 1 cup currants
- ½ cup shredded suet (vegetable suet for a vegetarian version)
- 1 cup sultanas (golden raisins)
- ½ cup chopped dried apricots
- ¼ teaspoon ground nutmeg
- ½ cup brandy or dark rum
- ¼ teaspoon ground cloves
- ½ cup dark brown sugar
- Zest and juice of 1 lemon
- ½ teaspoon ground cinnamon
- Zest and juice of 1 orange

For The Pie Crust:
- 2 cups all-purpose flour
- 1 large egg, beaten
- ½ cup unsalted butter, chilled and diced
- 1-2 tablespoons cold water (as needed)
- ¼ cup granulated sugar

Directions

For Mincemeat Filling:

1. In a large mixing bowl, combine the raisins, currants, sultanas, candied peel, dried apples, dried apricots, shredded suet, and dark brown sugar.
2. Add the brandy or dark rum, lemon zest, lemon juice, orange zest, orange juice, ground cinnamon, ground cloves, and ground nutmeg to the bowl. Mix well until all the ingredients are thoroughly combined.
3. Cover the bowl with a clean cloth or plastic wrap and let the mincemeat mixture rest for at least 24 hours. This allows the flavors to meld together.

For Pie Crust:

1. In a mixing bowl, combine the all-purpose flour, diced unsalted butter, and granulated sugar.
2. Rub the butter into the flour mixture using your fingertips until the mixture resembles breadcrumbs.
3. Add the beaten egg to the mixture and mix until the dough starts to come together. If the dough is too dry, add cold water, one tablespoon at a time, until the dough forms a ball.
4. On a lightly floured surface, roll out half of the pastry to fit a 9-inch pie dish.

Filling The Pie:

1. Place the rolled-out pastry in the pie dish.
2. Spoon the prepared mincemeat filling into the pastry-lined pie dish, spreading it evenly.
3. Roll out the remaining pastry to create the top crust. You can either place the whole rolled-out pastry on top of the mincemeat filling or create a lattice pattern using strips of pastry.
4. Trim any excess pastry from the edges and press the edges of the top and bottom crusts together to seal the pie.

Baking:

1. Preheat your oven to 375 F.
2. Bake the mince pie in the preheated oven for about 25-30 minutes or until the crust is golden brown.
3. Allow the mince pie to cool slightly before serving.

Confederate Johnny Cake from 1865

Prep: 20 minutes – Cook: 40 minutes – Servings: 10
Calories: 140 – Fat: 7g – Carbs: 14g – Fiber: 2g – Sugar: 1g – Protein: 2g

Confederate Johnny Cake, also known as Southern Johnny Cake or Hoecake, is a traditional American cornbread that has its roots in the Southern United States, including during the Civil War era in the 1860s. Johnny Cakes were a popular staple in Confederate households, as they were made using simple ingredients that were readily available. Confederate Johnny Cakes can be served as a savory side dish alongside various Southern dishes, such as fried chicken, collard greens, or black-eyed peas. For a sweeter twist, you can serve Johnny Cakes with honey, molasses, maple syrup, or your favorite fruit preserves.

Ingredients

- 1 cup cornmeal
- 2-3 tablespoons bacon drippings, lard, or vegetable oil (for frying)
- 1 cup boiling water
- ½ teaspoon salt

Directions

1. In a mixing bowl, combine the cornmeal and salt.
2. Pour the boiling water over the cornmeal mixture and stir until well combined. The mixture should form a thick batter.
3. Cover the bowl with a clean cloth or plastic wrap and let the batter rest for about 10-15 minutes.
4. Divide the batter into small portions and shape each portion into a flat, round cake, about 3-4 inches in diameter and 1/4 inch thick. You can make them thinner or thicker to your liking.
5. In a large skillet or griddle, heat the bacon drippings, lard, or vegetable oil over medium heat.
6. Once the fat is hot, carefully place the shaped Johnny Cakes in the skillet, making sure not to overcrowd the pan. Cook them in batches if needed.
7. Cook the Johnny Cakes for about 3-4 minutes on each side or until they are golden brown and crispy.
8. Transfer the cooked Johnny Cakes to a plate lined with paper towels to drain any excess oil.

Ginger Snaps From 1870

Prep: 20 minutes – Cook: 1 hour & 25 minutes – Servings: 36
Calories: 90 – Fat: 4g – Carbs: 10g – Fiber: 1g – Sugar: 6g – Protein: 2g

Ginger snaps, also known as ginger biscuits, are a classic and flavorful cookie that has been enjoyed for centuries. By the 1870s, ginger snaps were a popular treat in the United States and other parts of the world. These cookies are characterized by their spiced and slightly crunchy texture, making them a favorite for ginger lovers.

Ingredients

- 1 cup unsalted butter, softened
- 2 ¼ cups all-purpose flour
- 1 cup granulated sugar
- ¼ cup molasses
- 1 large egg
- ½ teaspoon baking soda
- 2 teaspoons ground ginger
- ½ teaspoon ground cloves
- 1 teaspoon ground cinnamon
- ¼ teaspoon salt
- Additional granulated sugar for rolling

Directions

1. Preheat your oven to 350 F. Line a baking sheet with parchment paper.
2. In a mixing bowl, cream together the softened unsalted butter and granulated sugar until light and fluffy.
3. Add the large egg to the butter and sugar mixture, beating well after each addition.
4. Stir in the molasses until well combined.
5. In a separate bowl, whisk together the all-purpose flour, ground ginger, ground cinnamon, ground cloves, baking soda, and salt.
6. Gradually add the dry ingredients to the wet ingredients, mixing until a smooth dough forms.
7. Wrap the dough in plastic wrap and refrigerate it for about 30 minutes to 1 hour. Chilling the dough helps with rolling and shaping the cookies.
8. Take small portions of the chilled dough and roll them into 1-inch balls. Roll each ball in granulated sugar to coat it completely.

9. Place the sugar-coated dough balls onto the prepared baking sheet, leaving some space between each cookie.
10. Use the bottom of a glass or a fork to gently flatten each dough ball to create the characteristic crinkled appearance of ginger snaps.
11. Bake the ginger snaps in the preheated oven for about 10-12 minutes or until the edges are slightly golden brown.
12. Remove the cookies from the oven and let them cool on the baking sheet for a few minutes before transferring them to a wire rack to cool completely.

Custard Pie From 1870

Prep: 20 minutes – Cook: 1 hour & 10 minutes – Servings: 10
Calories: 340 – Fat: 20g – Carbs: 39g – Fiber: 2g – Sugar: 20g – Protein: 4g

Custard pie was a popular and cherished dessert enjoyed in the United States and beyond. Custard pie is a simple, yet delightful pie made with a creamy custard filling, often flavored with vanilla or other flavorings, and baked in a flaky pie crust. It has been a classic dessert for generations and continues to be loved today.

Ingredients

For The Pie Crust:

- 2 cups all-purpose flour
- ½ cup unsalted butter, chilled and diced
- 1 large egg, beaten
- ¼ cup granulated sugar
- 1-2 tablespoons cold water (as needed)

For The Custard Filling:

- 1 ½ cups whole milk
- 4 large eggs
- 1 teaspoon vanilla extract
- ¾ cup granulated sugar
- A pinch of salt
- ½ cup heavy cream
- Ground nutmeg or ground cinnamon for sprinkling (optional)

Directions

For Pie Crust:

1. Preheat your oven to 375 F. Grease a 9-inch pie dish.
2. In a mixing bowl, combine the all-purpose flour, diced unsalted butter, and granulated sugar.
3. Rub the butter into the flour mixture using your fingertips until the mixture resembles breadcrumbs.
4. Add the beaten egg to the mixture and mix until the dough starts to come together. If the dough is too dry, add cold water, one tablespoon at a time, until the dough forms a ball.
5. On a lightly floured surface, roll out the pastry to fit the greased pie dish.
6. Carefully transfer the rolled-out pastry to the pie dish, pressing it gently into the edges and sides.
7. Trim any excess pastry from the edges of the pie dish. You can crimp the edges for a decorative touch if desired.

For Custard Filling:

1. In a saucepan, heat the whole milk and heavy cream over medium heat until it starts to simmer. Remove from heat and let it cool slightly.
2. In a separate mixing bowl, whisk together the eggs, granulated sugar, vanilla extract, and a pinch of salt.
3. Gradually add the warm milk mixture to the egg mixture, whisking continuously to prevent the eggs from curdling.
4. Strain the custard mixture through a fine-mesh sieve into a separate bowl to remove any lumps or curdled bits.

Assembling and Baking the Custard Pie:

1. Carefully pour the strained custard into the prepared pie crust.
2. Sprinkle a pinch of ground nutmeg or ground cinnamon on top of the custard for added flavor (optional).
3. Bake the custard pie in the preheated oven for about 30-35 minutes or until the custard is set around the edges but slightly wobbly in the center.
4. Remove the custard pie from the oven and let it cool completely on a wire rack. Once cooled, slice and serve the custard pie at room temperature. It can be enjoyed on its own or with a dollop of whipped cream on top.

Bakewell Tart From 1870

Prep: 20 minutes – Cook: 55 minutes – Servings: 10
Calories: 340 – Fat: 24g – Carbs: 34g – Fiber: 2g – Sugar: 24g – Protein: 4g

The Bakewell Tart is a traditional English dessert that has a long history. While the exact origins of the Bakewell Tart are somewhat disputed, it is believed to have evolved from the Bakewell Pudding, which is said to have been created accidentally by a cook in the town of Bakewell, Derbyshire, England. The tart typically consists of a short crust pastry shell filled with layers of jam and an almond frangipane filling, topped with a simple glaze, and sometimes adorned with flaked almonds.

Ingredients

For Shortcrust Pastry:
- ½ cup unsalted butter, chilled and diced
- 2 cups all-purpose flour
- 1-2 tablespoons cold water (as needed)
- 1 large egg, beaten
- ¼ cup granulated sugar

For Almond Frangipane Filling:
- 1 cup ground almonds
- 2 large eggs
- 1 teaspoon almond extract
- ¼ cup unsalted butter, softened
- 1-2 tablespoons all-purpose flour
- ½ cup granulated sugar

For Jam Layer:
- ½ cup raspberry jam (traditional choice, but you can use other fruit jams of your preference)

For Glaze & Garnish:
- 1-2 tablespoons water
- ¼ cup powdered sugar (icing sugar)
- Flaked almonds for decoration (optional)

Directions

For Shortcrust Pastry:

1. Preheat your oven to 375 F. Grease a 9-inch tart tin or pie dish.
2. In a mixing bowl, combine the all-purpose flour, diced unsalted butter, and granulated sugar.
3. Rub the butter into the flour mixture using your fingertips until the mixture resembles breadcrumbs.
4. Add the beaten egg to the mixture and mix until the dough starts to come together. If the dough is too dry, add cold water, one tablespoon at a time, until the dough forms a ball.
5. On a lightly floured surface, roll out the pastry to fit the greased tart tin or pie dish.
6. Carefully transfer the rolled-out pastry to the tart tin or pie dish, pressing it gently into the edges and sides.
7. Trim any excess pastry from the edges of the tin or dish. You can crimp the edges for a decorative touch if desired.

For the Almond Frangipane Filling:

1. In a mixing bowl, cream together the softened unsalted butter and granulated sugar until light and fluffy.
2. Gradually add the ground almonds to the butter and sugar mixture, mixing until well combined.
3. Beat in the eggs, one at a time, followed by the almond extract.
4. Gradually add the all-purpose flour to the mixture and mix until the filling thickens slightly.

Assembling and Baking the Bakewell Tart:

1. Spread the raspberry jam evenly over the bottom of the prepared pastry shell.
2. Spoon the almond frangipane filling over the jam layer, spreading it out evenly.
3. Bake the Bakewell Tart in the preheated oven for about 30-35 minutes or until the filling is set and golden brown.

For the Glaze and Garnish:

1. In a small bowl, mix the powdered sugar with enough water to create a smooth glaze.
2. Once the tart is out of the oven and slightly cooled, drizzle the glaze over the top of the tart.
3. Optionally, decorate the Bakewell Tart with flaked almonds on top of the glaze for an attractive finish.
4. Allow the Bakewell Tart to cool completely before serving. It can be enjoyed at room temperature.

Baked Alaska from 1875

Prep: 20 minutes – Cook: 55 minutes – Servings: 6
Calories: 340 – Fat: 16g – Carbs: 40g – Fiber: 2g – Sugar: 34g – Protein: 4g

Baked Alaska is a show-stopping dessert that features a layer of cake, a layer of ice cream, and a fluffy meringue coating. The meringue is then browned and crisped using high heat, creating a stunning contrast between the toasted exterior and the cold ice cream within. Instead of using just ice cream as the filling, you can add a layer of fresh or frozen fruits between the cake and the ice cream. Popular choices include sliced strawberries, raspberries, blueberries, or a combination of fruits. This addition will add a burst of fruity flavor to the dessert.

Ingredients

- 1 pound cake or sponge cake (store-bought or homemade)
- ½ teaspoon cream of tartar
- 1 quart (4 cups) ice cream (flavor of your choice)
- 6 large egg whites, at room temperature
- 1 teaspoon vanilla extract
- ½ cup granulated sugar

Directions

For Cake Base:
1. Preheat your oven to 400 F.
2. Cut the pound cake or sponge cake into a shape that fits the base of your serving dish or pan. You can cut it into rounds, squares, or any other desired shape.
3. Place the cake layer at the bottom of the serving dish or pan.

For Ice Cream Layer:
1. Take the ice cream out of the freezer and let it soften slightly at room temperature for about 5-10 minutes. This will make it easier to spread.
2. Spread the softened ice cream evenly over the cake layer in the serving dish or pan. Smooth the surface with a spatula.
3. Place the dish or pan with the cake and ice cream in the freezer for at least 1-2 hours or until the ice cream is firm.

For Meringue Topping:
1. In a clean mixing bowl, beat the egg whites and cream of tartar with an electric mixer on medium speed until frothy.
2. Gradually add the granulated sugar to the egg whites while continuing to beat. Beat until stiff peaks form and the meringue is glossy.
3. Gently fold in the vanilla extract until well incorporated.

Assembling and Baking the Baked Alaska:
1. Remove the cake and ice cream from the freezer. Working quickly, spread the meringue over the entire surface of the ice cream, making sure to cover it completely and seal the edges.
2. Use the back of a spoon or a spatula to create decorative swirls or peaks on the meringue. This will help the meringue brown beautifully in the oven.
3. Place the assembled Baked Alaska in the preheated oven and bake for about 5-7 minutes or until the meringue is lightly browned.
4. Remove the Baked Alaska from the oven and serve immediately.

Zucchini Bread From 1875

Prep: 20 minutes – Cook: 1 hour & 25 minutes – Servings: 10
Calories: 240 – Fat: 14g – Carbs: 30g – Fiber: 2g – Sugar: 16g – Protein: 4g

Zucchini, also known as courgette, is a type of summer squash that originated in the Americas but only became widely known in Europe and North America. To create a historical-inspired squash bread recipe from around the 1870s, we can adapt an old pumpkin bread recipe and use zucchini as a substitute. Dried fruits were commonly used in historical baking, and they add natural sweetness and chewiness to the bread. The combination of raisins, currants, and chopped dried apricots creates a medley of flavors and textures.

Ingredients

- 1 ½ cups all-purpose flour
- ½ teaspoon baking powder
- 2 cups zucchini, grated
- ½ cup whole wheat flour
- 1 teaspoon baking soda
- ¼ teaspoon ground cloves
- 1 teaspoon ground cinnamon
- ½ cup unsalted butter, melted
- 1 cup granulated sugar
- ½ teaspoon ground nutmeg
- 2 large eggs
- ½ cup chopped walnuts or pecans (optional)
- 1 teaspoon vanilla extract
- ½ teaspoon salt

Directions

1. Preheat your oven to 350 F. Grease and flour a 9x5-inch loaf pan.
2. Grate the zucchini using a box grater or a food processor with the grating attachment. Squeeze out excess moisture from the grated zucchini using a clean cloth or paper towels.
3. In a mixing bowl, whisk together the all-purpose flour, whole wheat flour, baking soda, baking powder, salt, ground cinnamon, ground nutmeg, and ground cloves.
4. In a separate large mixing bowl, whisk together the granulated sugar, melted butter, eggs, and vanilla extract until well combined.
5. Gradually add the grated zucchini to the wet ingredients, stirring until evenly distributed.
6. If using nuts, fold in the chopped walnuts or pecans into the zucchini mixture.
7. Gently fold the dry flour mixture into the zucchini mixture until just combined. Be careful not to overmix the batter.
8. Pour the batter into the prepared loaf pan and spread it evenly.
9. Bake in the preheated oven for approximately 50-60 minutes or until a toothpick inserted into the center comes out clean.
10. Remove the zucchini bread from the oven and let it cool in the pan for about 10 minutes before transferring it to a wire rack to cool completely.

Apple Dumplings From 1875

Prep: 2 minutes – Cook: 1 hour & 25 minutes – Servings: 4
Calories: 400 – Fat: 24g – Carbs: 49g – Fiber: 2g – Sugar: 24g – Protein: 3g

Apple dumplings have a long history in American cuisine and were enjoyed by families in the 19th century, including in 1875. These delightful desserts consist of spiced apples wrapped in pastry and baked until tender and golden. Tart apples, such as Granny Smith, work well in this recipe as their acidity complements the sweetness of the sugar-spice filling.

Ingredients

For The Pastry:

- 2 cups all-purpose flour
- 2/3 cup unsalted butter, chilled and diced
- 4-6 tablespoons ice water
- 1 teaspoon salt

For The Apple Filling:

- ½ cup granulated sugar
- 4 medium-sized tart apples (such as Granny Smith)
- ¼ teaspoon ground nutmeg
- 1 teaspoon ground cinnamon
- ¼ teaspoon ground cloves
- 2 tablespoons unsalted butter, cut into 4 pieces
- 1 tablespoon lemon juice

For The Syrup:

- ½ teaspoon ground cinnamon
- 1 cup water
- ¼ teaspoon ground nutmeg
- 1 cup granulated sugar
- ¼ cup unsalted butter

Directions

For The Pastry:
1. In a mixing bowl, whisk together the all-purpose flour and salt.
2. Add the chilled diced unsalted butter to the flour mixture.
3. Using a pastry cutter or your fingertips, cut the butter into the flour until the mixture resembles coarse crumbs.
4. Gradually add ice water, one tablespoon at a time, and mix until the dough comes together. Be careful not to overwork the dough.
5. Form the pastry into a ball, wrap it in plastic wrap, and refrigerate for at least 30 minutes.

For the Apple Filling:
1. Preheat your oven to 375 F.
2. Peel, core, and halve the apples.
3. In a small bowl, mix together the granulated sugar, ground cinnamon, ground nutmeg, and ground cloves.
4. Sprinkle the sugar-spice mixture over the cut sides of the apple halves, and drizzle them with lemon juice.

Assembling Dumplings:
1. Take each apple half and place one piece of butter in the center. Bring the edges of the pastry up and over the apple, sealing it completely.

For the Syrup:
1. In a saucepan, combine water, granulated sugar, ground cinnamon, ground nutmeg, and unsalted butter.
2. Bring the syrup mixture to a boil over medium heat, stirring until the sugar has dissolved.

Baking the Apple Dumplings:
1. Place the assembled dumplings in a baking dish.
2. Pour the hot syrup over the dumplings, making sure they are evenly coated.
3. Bake the apple dumplings in the preheated oven for about 40-45 minutes or until the pastry is golden brown, and the apples are tender.
4. Remove the apple dumplings from the oven and serve them warm. They can be enjoyed on their own or served with a scoop of vanilla ice cream or a drizzle of heavy cream.

Meringue Pie From 1875

Prep: 20 minutes – Cook: 55 minutes – Servings: 8
Calories: 340 – Fat: 16g – Carbs: 44g – Fiber: 2g – Sugar: 24g – Protein: 4g

Meringue pies have a long history and were enjoyed in the 19th century, including in 1875. These pies typically feature a sweet and fluffy meringue topping over a delicious filling, such as lemon or chocolate. For a delicious twist, turn this into a Chocolate Meringue Pie by adding melted chocolate to the lemon filling. Simply melt some semi-sweet or dark chocolate and stir it into the lemon filling after it has thickened. The combination of tangy lemon and rich chocolate is divine.

Ingredients

For The Pie Crust:
- ½ cup unsalted butter, chilled and diced
- 1 ¼ cups all-purpose flour
- ¼ cup ice water
- ¼ teaspoon salt

For The Lemon Filling:
- ¼ cup cornstarch
- 1 cup granulated sugar
- ½ cup fresh lemon juice
- 3 large egg yolks, lightly beaten
- 1 ½ cups water
- Zest of 1 lemon
- 2 tablespoons unsalted butter
- ¼ teaspoon salt

For The Meringue Topping:
- ¼ teaspoon cream of tartar
- 4 large egg whites, at room temperature
- ½ teaspoon vanilla extract
- ½ cup granulated sugar

Directions

For The Pie Crust:
1. In a mixing bowl, whisk together the all-purpose flour and salt.
2. Add the chilled diced unsalted butter to the flour mixture.

3. Using a pastry cutter or your fingertips, cut the butter into the flour until the mixture resembles coarse crumbs.
4. Gradually add ice water, one tablespoon at a time, and mix until the dough comes together. Be careful not to overwork the dough.
5. Form the dough into a ball, wrap it in plastic wrap, and refrigerate for at least 30 minutes.

For the Lemon Filling:
1. Preheat your oven to 375 F.
2. In a saucepan, whisk together the granulated sugar, cornstarch, and salt. Gradually stir in the water.
3. Cook the sugar-water mixture over medium heat, stirring constantly until it thickens and becomes clear.
4. Gradually whisk a small amount of the hot sugar-water mixture into the beaten egg yolks. This is called "tempering" and prevents the eggs from curdling.
5. Return the egg yolk mixture to the saucepan and continue cooking, stirring constantly, until the filling thickens to a pudding-like consistency.
6. Remove the saucepan from the heat and stir in the fresh lemon juice, lemon zest, and unsalted butter until the butter is fully melted and incorporated.

Assembling and Baking the Pie:
1. On a floured surface, roll out the chilled pie crust to fit a 9-inch pie dish. Transfer the crust to the pie dish, trim the excess, and crimp the edges.
2. Pour the lemon filling into the prepared pie crust, spreading it evenly.
3. In a clean mixing bowl, beat the egg whites and cream of tartar with an electric mixer on medium speed until frothy.
4. Gradually add the granulated sugar to the egg whites while continuing to beat. Beat until stiff peaks form and the meringue is glossy.
5. Gently fold in the vanilla extract until well incorporated.
6. Spread the meringue over the lemon filling, making sure to seal the edges.
7. Bake the pie in the preheated oven for about 10-12 minutes or until the meringue is lightly browned.
8. Remove the pie from the oven and let it cool completely before serving.

Parker House Rolls From 1880

Prep: 20 minutes – Cook: 2 hours & 25 minutes – Servings: 12
Calories: 160 – Fat: 6g – Carbs: 22g – Fiber: 1g – Sugar: 4g – Protein: 3g

Parker House Rolls are a classic type of soft, buttery dinner roll that originated at the Parker House Hotel in Boston in the 19th century. The hotel, which opened in 1855, became well-known for these delectable rolls, and they have remained a beloved American staple ever since. Parker House Rolls are traditionally shaped as half-moons, a shape said to originate from a playful accident at the Parker House Hotel in Boston.

Ingredients

- ¼ cup granulated sugar
- 2 ¼ teaspoons active dry yeast (1 packet)
- ¼ cup unsalted butter, melted and slightly cooled
- 1 cup warm milk (110 F)
- ½ cup warm water
- 4 cups all-purpose flour
- 1 teaspoon salt
- ¼ cup unsalted butter, melted (for brushing)

Directions

1. In a small bowl, dissolve the granulated sugar in warm water. Sprinkle the yeast over the water and let it sit for about 5 minutes until it becomes foamy.
2. In a large mixing bowl, combine the warm milk, melted butter, and salt. Add the foamy yeast mixture to the bowl and mix well.
3. Gradually add the all-purpose flour to the liquid mixture, stirring with a wooden spoon until a soft dough forms.
4. Turn the dough out onto a lightly floured surface and knead it for about 5-7 minutes until it becomes smooth and elastic.

First Rise:

1. Place the dough in a greased bowl, cover it with a clean kitchen towel, and let it rise in a warm place for about 1 to 1 ½ hours, or until it doubles in size.

Shaping the Rolls:

1. Preheat your oven to 375 F. Grease a 9x13-inch baking dish.
2. Punch down the risen dough and turn it out onto a lightly floured surface. Roll it out to a thickness of about 1/2 inch.
3. Using a round biscuit cutter or a drinking glass, cut the dough into circles. Then, fold each circle in half to create a half-moon shape.
4. Place the shaped rolls in the greased baking dish, arranging them closely together.

Second Rise:

1. Cover the baking dish with a clean kitchen towel and let the rolls rise for another 30-45 minutes, until they are puffy and have expanded.

Baking the Rolls:

1. Bake the rolls in the preheated oven for about 15-18 minutes or until they turn golden brown on top.
2. Remove the rolls from the oven and immediately brush the tops with the melted butter while they are still warm.

Blancmange From 1880

Prep: 20 minutes – Cook: 3 hours & 25 minutes – Servings: 6
Calories: 240 – Fat: 7g – Carbs: 34g – Fiber: 1g – Sugar: 24g – Protein: 6g

Blancmange, pronounced "bluh-mahnj," is a classic dessert with a long history, and it was particularly popular in the 19th century, including in 1880. Blancmange is a sweet, creamy, and delicately flavored dessert that is thickened with cornstarch or gelatin. It can be flavored with various ingredients, such as almonds, vanilla, or rosewater. If you want a more traditional flavor, you can use rosewater instead of vanilla extract. Rosewater adds a floral and aromatic note to the blancmange.

Ingredients

- 4 cups whole milk
- ½ cup granulated sugar
- 1 teaspoon vanilla extract (or 1 tablespoon rosewater for a different flavor)
- ½ cup cornstarch
- Sliced almonds, for garnish (optional)
- ½ cup blanched almonds, finely ground (or almond flour)
- Fresh berries or fruit compote, for serving (optional)

Directions

1. In a saucepan, warm the whole milk over medium heat until it is steaming. Do not boil the milk.
2. Add the finely ground blanched almonds to the warm milk and let it steep for about 30 minutes. This will infuse the milk with a subtle almond flavor.
3. After 30 minutes, strain the almond-infused milk through a fine-mesh sieve or cheesecloth to remove the almond solids. Return the strained milk to the saucepan.
4. In a separate bowl, whisk the cornstarch with a small amount of water to make a slurry. Make sure there are no lumps in the mixture.
5. Add the sugar to the almond-infused milk and warm it over medium-low heat. Gradually stir in the cornstarch slurry, stirring constantly to prevent lumps.
6. Continue stirring until the mixture thickens to a smooth and creamy consistency. This may take about 5-7 minutes.
7. Remove the saucepan from the heat and stir in the vanilla extract (or rosewater, if using) to add a delightful flavor to the blancmange.
8. Pour the blancmange into individual serving dishes or a large mold. If using individual molds, lightly grease them with a little vegetable oil before pouring in the mixture.
9. Allow the blancmange to cool to room temperature before refrigerating it for at least 2-3 hours, or until it is fully set.
10. Once fully set, garnish the blancmange with sliced almonds, if desired. You can also serve it with fresh berries or a fruit compote for a delightful accompaniment.

Charlotte Russe From 1880

Prep: 20 minutes – Cook: 4 hours & 25 minutes – Servings: 6
Calories: 240 – Fat: 24g – Carbs: 16g – Fiber: 2g – Sugar: 14g – Protein: 3g

Charlotte Russe is a classic dessert that was particularly popular in the late 19th century, including around 1880. It is a type of chilled dessert made with ladyfingers (sponge cake or biscuit), filled with a light and fluffy mousse-like mixture, often containing whipped cream and fruit. The dessert is then set in a mold or served in individual glasses. Use fresh seasonal fruit of your choice for a delightful burst of flavor. Strawberries, raspberries, and peaches are traditional choices.

Ingredients

- 1 tablespoon gelatin (or 1 tablespoon powdered agar-agar for a vegetarian version)
- 1 ½ cups heavy cream, chilled
- 1 teaspoon vanilla extract
- 2 cups fresh fruit (such as strawberries, raspberries, or peaches), diced or sliced
- ½ cup granulated sugar
- 24-30 ladyfingers (sponge cake or biscuit type)
- ¼ cup cold water
- Sliced almonds or chocolate shavings, for garnish (optional)

Directions

1. In a large mixing bowl, whip the chilled heavy cream with an electric mixer until soft peaks form.
2. Gradually add the granulated sugar and vanilla extract to the whipped cream while continuing to beat. Whip until stiff peaks form. Set the whipped cream aside.
3. In a small bowl, sprinkle the gelatin over cold water and let it sit for about 5 minutes to soften.
4. If using agar-agar, follow the package instructions to dissolve it in water.
5. Place the softened gelatin (or dissolved agar-agar) in a saucepan over low heat. Gently warm it, stirring constantly, until it completely dissolves. Be careful not to boil the gelatin.
6. Gradually fold the warm gelatin (or agar-agar) into the whipped cream mixture until well incorporated. The gelatin will help set the dessert.
7. Gently fold the diced or sliced fresh fruit into the whipped cream mixture. Reserve some fruit for garnishing the top.
8. Line the bottom and sides of a large mold or individual glasses with the ladyfingers, positioning them vertically and closely together.
9. Pour the whipped cream and fruit mixture into the lined mold or glasses, making sure it fills all the spaces.
10. Refrigerate the Charlotte Russe for at least 4 hours, or preferably overnight, to allow it to set and develop its flavors.
11. Before serving, garnish the Charlotte Russe with additional sliced fruit, sliced almonds, or chocolate shavings, if desired.

Banana Fritters From 1885

Prep: 20 minutes – Cook: 35 minutes – Servings: 12
Calories: 80 – Fat: 4g – Carbs: 12g – Fiber: 1g – Sugar: 6g – Protein: 1g

Banana fritters are a delicious and timeless treat enjoyed in various cultures around the world. In 1885, these delectable fritters were likely made using simple and readily available ingredients. Make sure to use ripe bananas with yellow skin and some brown spots. They are sweeter and will add more flavor to the fritters.

Ingredients

- 2-3 ripe bananas (yellow with some brown spots), peeled and sliced
- 1 cup all-purpose flour
- 2 tablespoons granulated sugar
- ½ teaspoon baking powder
- A pinch of salt
- ½ cup milk
- 1 large egg
- Vegetable oil, for frying
- Powdered sugar, for dusting (optional)
- Honey or maple syrup, for drizzling (optional)

Directions

1. Peel the ripe bananas and cut them into slices, approximately 1/2 inch thick. Set aside.
2. In a mixing bowl, combine the all-purpose flour, granulated sugar, baking powder, and a pinch of salt.
3. In a separate bowl, whisk together the milk and egg until well combined.
4. Gradually pour the milk and egg mixture into the dry ingredients, stirring until you achieve a smooth batter. The batter should be thick enough to coat the back of a spoon.
5. In a deep skillet or frying pan, heat vegetable oil over medium-high heat. The oil should be deep enough to submerge the banana slices.
6. Once the oil is hot, dip each banana slice into the batter, coating it evenly, and carefully place it in the hot oil.
7. Fry the banana fritters in batches, being careful not to overcrowd the pan. Fry them until they turn golden brown on both sides, about 2-3 minutes per side.
8. Use a slotted spoon to remove the fried banana fritters from the oil and place them on a plate lined with paper towels to drain any excess oil.
9. While the fritters are still warm, you can dust them with powdered sugar for added sweetness.
10. For an indulgent touch, drizzle honey or maple syrup over the fritters before serving.
11. Banana fritters are best enjoyed warm and fresh. Serve them as a delightful dessert or snack, perfect for a sweet treat at any time of the day.

Buttermilk Biscuits From 1885

Prep: 20 minutes – Cook: 45 minutes – Servings: 10
Calories: 120 – Fat: 6g – Carbs: 16g – Fiber: 1g – Sugar: 2g – Protein: 2g

Buttermilk biscuits were a popular and simple staple in many households. Buttermilk biscuits are light, fluffy, and slightly tangy, thanks to the addition of buttermilk. They can be served as a delightful accompaniment to meals, especially breakfast, or enjoyed on their own with a pat of butter or jam. For different flavor variations, you can add grated cheese, herbs (such as chives or rosemary), or even spices (like cinnamon or nutmeg) to the flour mixture before adding the buttermilk. Experiment with different flavors to suit your taste preferences.

Ingredients

- ¼ cup cold unsalted butter, cut into small cubes
- 2 cups all-purpose flour
- ½ teaspoon baking soda
- 2 teaspoons baking powder
- ¾ cup buttermilk (cold)
- 1 tablespoon granulated sugar (optional, for a touch of sweetness)
- ½ teaspoon salt

Directions

1. Preheat your oven to 450 F. Adjust the oven rack to the center position.
2. In a large mixing bowl, whisk together the all-purpose flour, baking powder, baking soda, salt, and granulated sugar (if using).
3. Add the cold, cubed unsalted butter to the dry ingredients. Using a pastry cutter or your fingers, cut the butter into the flour mixture until it resembles coarse crumbs.
4. Pour the cold buttermilk into the flour mixture. Stir gently with a fork until the ingredients come together to form a soft dough. Be careful not to overmix the dough.
5. Turn the dough out onto a lightly floured surface. Gently knead the dough a few times until it becomes smooth. Avoid excessive kneading, as this could make the biscuits tough.
6. Roll the dough out to a thickness of about 3/4 inch. Using a round biscuit cutter or a drinking glass, cut the dough into circles.
7. Place the biscuits on an ungreased baking sheet, spacing them slightly apart.
8. Bake the biscuits in the preheated oven for approximately 12-15 minutes, or until they turn golden brown on top.
9. Serve the buttermilk biscuits warm, either plain or with a spread of butter, jam, or honey.

Victoria Sandwich Cake From 1890

Prep: 10 minutes – Cook: 50 minutes – Servings: 10
Calories: 360 – Fat: 24g – Carbs: 39g – Fiber: 1g – Sugar: 24g – Protein: 4g

The Victoria Sandwich Cake, also known as Victoria Sponge Cake, is a classic and iconic British cake that was named after Queen Victoria. It became popular during the late 19th century, including in 1890. The cake consists of two layers of sponge cake sandwiched together with jam and whipped cream. It is a simple yet delightful cake that celebrates the beauty of simplicity and the wonderful flavors of jam and cream. To help the whipped cream hold its shape, you can add a stabilizer, such as gelatin or cornstarch, to the cream while whipping.

Ingredients

For The Sponge Cake Layers:
- 4 large eggs, at room temperature
- 1 cup granulated sugar
- 2 cups all-purpose flour
- 1 cup (2 sticks) unsalted butter, softened
- 2 teaspoons baking powder
- ½ cup milk, at room temperature
- 1 teaspoon vanilla extract
- ½ teaspoon salt

For The Filling:
- 1 teaspoon vanilla extract
- Raspberry or strawberry jam (or any jam of your choice)
- 2 tablespoons powdered sugar
- 1 cup heavy cream, chilled

Directions

1. Preheat your oven to 350 F. Grease two 8-inch round cake pans and line the bottoms with parchment paper.
2. In a large mixing bowl, cream together the softened butter and granulated sugar until light and fluffy.
3. Beat in the eggs, one at a time, until well incorporated. Add the vanilla extract and mix until combined.
4. In a separate bowl, whisk together the all-purpose flour, baking powder, and salt.
5. Gradually add the dry ingredients to the butter mixture, alternating with the milk. Start and end with the dry ingredients, mixing after each addition until just combined. Be careful not to overmix.
6. Divide the cake batter evenly between the prepared cake pans.
7. Bake the cake layers in the preheated oven for about 20-25 minutes or until a toothpick inserted into the center of the cakes comes out clean.
8. Remove the cakes from the oven and let them cool in the pans for a few minutes before transferring them to wire racks to cool completely.
9. In a chilled mixing bowl, whip the heavy cream with an electric mixer until it starts to thicken.
10. Gradually add the powdered sugar and vanilla extract to the whipped cream. Continue whipping until stiff peaks form.
11. Once the cake layers have cooled, spread a layer of jam on the top of one of the cake layers.
12. Carefully spread a generous layer of whipped cream over the jam.
13. Place the second cake layer on top, creating a sandwich.
14. Optionally, you can dust the top of the cake with powdered sugar for a decorative touch. Cut the Victoria Sandwich Cake into slices and serve it with a cup of tea or as a delightful treat for any special occasion or afternoon tea.

Tapioca Pudding From 1890

Prep: 20 minutes – Cook: 45 minutes – Servings: 4
Calories: 240 – Fat: 10g – Carbs: 40g – Fiber: 1g – Sugar: 30g – Protein: 6g

Tapioca pudding is a classic and comforting dessert that has been enjoyed for centuries, including during the late 19th century, around 1890. Tapioca pearls are cooked in milk until they become soft and translucent, creating a creamy and delicious pudding. You can consider using low-fat milk, reducing the sugar, or using alternative sweeteners.

Ingredients

- ½ cup granulated sugar
- 2 ½ cups whole milk
- ½ cup small pearl tapioca
- 2 large egg yolks
- ½ teaspoon vanilla extract
- Ground cinnamon or nutmeg (for garnish)
- ¼ teaspoon salt

Directions

1. Rinse the tapioca: Place the tapioca pearls in a fine-mesh strainer and rinse them under cold water. This helps to remove any excess starch.
2. Soak the tapioca: In a bowl, combine the rinsed tapioca with 1 cup of water and let it soak for about 30 minutes. After soaking, drain any remaining water.
3. Cook the tapioca: In a medium-sized saucepan, combine the soaked tapioca, 2 cups of whole milk, and salt. Place the saucepan over medium heat and bring the mixture to a simmer while stirring constantly to prevent sticking. Reduce the heat to low and let it cook for about 10-15 minutes, or until the tapioca pearls are translucent and soft.
4. Prepare the custard: In a separate bowl, whisk the egg yolks and sugar until they are well combined. Gradually add the remaining 1/2 cup of whole milk to the egg mixture while continuously whisking.
5. Combine the custard with tapioca: Slowly pour the egg and milk mixture into the saucepan with the cooked tapioca while stirring constantly. Continue to cook over low heat, stirring gently, for an additional 5 minutes to thicken the pudding.
6. Add vanilla: Remove the saucepan from the heat and stir in the vanilla extract. This gives the pudding a lovely flavor.
7. Chill and serve: Transfer the tapioca pudding into individual serving bowls or a large dish. Let it cool to room temperature, then cover and refrigerate until chilled and set. Before serving, you can sprinkle a bit of ground cinnamon or nutmeg on top for added flavor and visual appeal.

Croissants From 1890

Prep: 20 minutes – Cook: 3 hours & 15 minutes – Servings: 10
Calories: 220 – Fat: 14g – Carbs: 20g – Fiber: 1g – Sugar: 9g – Protein: 4g

Croissants have a fascinating history that goes back to the 17th century in Austria. However, the modern version of the croissant, as we know it today, is believed to have been perfected in France in the late 1800s, particularly during the Belle Époque era. Croissants are best enjoyed fresh on the day they are made. If you have leftovers, you can store them in an airtight container at room temperature for a day or two, but they are at their peak when fresh.

Ingredients

- 2 cups all-purpose flour
- 1 teaspoon active dry yeast
- ½ cup milk
- 1 cup unsalted butter, cold
- ¼ cup granulated sugar
- 1 large egg (for egg wash)
- ¼ cup water
- Powdered sugar (for dusting)
- ½ teaspoon salt

Directions

1. Activate the yeast: In a small bowl, combine the yeast with warm water (about 110 F) and a pinch of sugar. Let it sit for about 5 minutes until the mixture becomes frothy.
2. Prepare the dough: In a large mixing bowl, combine the flour, sugar, and salt. Make a well in the center and pour in the activated yeast and milk. Mix everything together until a dough forms.
3. Knead the dough: Transfer the dough onto a floured surface and knead it for about 5-7 minutes until it becomes smooth and elastic.
4. Incorporate the butter: Roll out the dough into a rectangle. Place the cold butter in the center and fold the sides of the dough over the butter, encasing it completely.
5. Create layers: Roll out the dough again into a rectangle, and then fold it into thirds like a letter. This process creates layers in the dough. Wrap the dough in plastic wrap and refrigerate for 30 minutes.
6. Repeat the folding: Take the dough out of the fridge, unwrap it, and repeat the rolling and folding process (rolling into a rectangle, folding into thirds). Refrigerate for another 30 minutes.
7. Shape the croissants: Roll out the dough one last time into a large rectangle and then cut it into triangles. Gently stretch each triangle and roll it up from the wide end to the pointed end, shaping it into a croissant.
8. Final rise: Place the shaped croissants on a baking sheet lined with parchment paper. Cover them loosely with a clean kitchen towel and let them rise for 1-2 hours or until they have doubled in size.
9. Preheat and egg wash: Preheat your oven to 400 F. In a small bowl, whisk the egg, and then brush the egg wash over the croissants gently.
10. Bake: Bake the croissants in the preheated oven for 15-20 minutes or until they are golden brown and flaky.
11. Serve: Once the croissants have cooled slightly, dust them with powdered sugar and serve.

Devil's Food Cake From 1895

Prep: 20 minutes – Cook: 50 minutes – Servings: 12
Calories: 400 – Fat: 20g – Carbs: 54g – Fiber: 2g – Sugar: 40g – Protein: 4g

Devil's Food Cake is a classic American chocolate cake that has been enjoyed for many years. While the exact origin of the cake's name is uncertain, it is believed to have been introduced in the late 19th century. Once the cakes are cooled, you can frost them with your favorite frosting. A traditional Devil's Food Cake is often frosted with a rich chocolate frosting or a creamy buttercream. It's meant to be enjoyed as an occasional treat rather than an everyday dessert. If you're looking to make a healthier version of Devil's Food Cake, you can consider using alternatives to some ingredients, like reducing the amount of sugar, using whole wheat flour, or incorporating healthier fats like avocado or coconut oil.

Ingredients

- 2 cups granulated sugar
- 1 cup (2 sticks) unsalted butter, at room temperature
- 3 large eggs
- 1 teaspoon vanilla extract
- ½ teaspoon baking soda
- 2 ½ cups all-purpose flour
- ½ cup cocoa powder
- 1 teaspoon baking powder
- ½ cup boiling water
- 1 cup buttermilk
- ½ teaspoon salt

Directions

1. Preheat your oven to 350 F. Grease and flour two 9-inch round cake pans.
2. In a large mixing bowl, cream the butter and sugar together until light and fluffy.
3. Beat in the eggs, one at a time, until well combined. Stir in the vanilla extract.
4. In a separate bowl, sift together the flour, cocoa powder, baking powder, baking soda, and salt.
5. Gradually add the dry ingredients to the butter mixture, alternating with the buttermilk. Begin and end with the dry ingredients, mixing until just combined after each addition.
6. Stir in the boiling water, ensuring the batter is well mixed but not over-mixed.
7. Divide the batter evenly between the prepared cake pans.
8. Bake in the preheated oven for about 25-30 minutes or until a toothpick inserted into the center of the cakes comes out clean.
9. Remove the cakes from the oven and let them cool in the pans for about 10 minutes. Then, transfer them to a wire rack to cool completely before frosting.

Eclairs From 1895

Prep: 20 minutes – Cook: 1 hour & 10 minutes – Servings: 12
Calories: 240 – Fat: 14g – Carbs: 24g – Fiber: 2g – Sugar: 16g – Protein: 4g

The classic éclair recipe from 1895 remains a beloved favorite. Instead of the classic vanilla whipped cream, try experimenting with different flavored fillings like chocolate ganache, coffee cream, fruit-flavored creams (such as raspberry or lemon), or even unique combinations like salted caramel or pistachio. Fruit-Topped Eclairs: After filling the eclairs, you can top them with fresh fruits like strawberries, raspberries, or blueberries to add a burst of color and natural sweetness.

Ingredients

For Choux Pastry:
- ¼ cup unsalted butter (½ stick)
- 2 large eggs
- ½ cup all-purpose flour
- A pinch of salt
- ½ cup water

For Filling:
- 1 cup heavy cream
- 2 tablespoons powdered sugar
- 1 teaspoon vanilla extract

For Chocolate Glaze:
- ¼ cup powdered sugar
- 2 tablespoons unsalted butter
- ½ cup semisweet chocolate chips or chopped chocolate
- 2-3 tablespoons hot water

Directions

1. Preheat your oven to 375 F. Line a baking sheet with parchment paper.
2. In a saucepan, combine the water, butter, and salt. Bring the mixture to a boil over medium heat.
3. Remove the saucepan from heat and quickly stir in the flour until the mixture forms a smooth ball of dough.
4. Add the eggs, one at a time, and mix well after each addition until the dough is smooth and glossy.
5. Transfer the choux pastry dough to a pastry bag fitted with a plain round tip.
6. Pipe the dough onto the prepared baking sheet in 3- to 4-inch-long strips, leaving space between each eclair.
7. Bake in the preheated oven for about 20-25 minutes or until the eclairs are golden brown and puffed up. Then, reduce the oven temperature to 325 F and continue baking for an additional 10-15 minutes to dry out the insides. Allow the eclairs to cool completely.
8. For the filling, whip the heavy cream, powdered sugar, and vanilla extract together until stiff peaks form. Transfer the whipped cream to a pastry bag fitted with a small round tip.
9. Once the eclairs are cooled, use the tip to make a small hole on the side of each eclair.
10. Pipe the whipped cream into each eclair through the hole until they are filled.
11. For the chocolate glaze, melt the chocolate and butter together in a microwave or using a double boiler.
12. Stir in the powdered sugar and enough hot water to create a smooth, pourable glaze.
13. Dip the tops of the filled eclairs into the chocolate glaze, allowing any excess to drip off.
14. Let the chocolate glaze set before serving the eclairs.

Opera Cake From 1895

Prep: 20 minutes – Cook: 2 hours & 20 minutes – Servings: 12
Calories: 444 – Fat: 34g – Carbs: 40g – Fiber: 3g – Sugar: 26g – Protein: 4g

The Opera Cake is a sophisticated and elegant dessert consisting of layers of almond sponge cake (Joconde), coffee-flavored buttercream, and chocolate ganache. It is typically finished with a chocolate glaze on top. The dessert is named after the Paris Opera House (Opéra Garnier) because its appearance is said to resemble the black and gold colors of the opera's interior. Incorporate fresh fruits like raspberries, strawberries, or sliced bananas between the layers of the cake for a burst of fruity flavor. You can also use fruit-flavored buttercream or ganache to complement the fruit filling.

Ingredients

For the Joconde Sponge:
- 1 cup almond flour
- ½ cup all-purpose flour
- 1 cup powdered sugar
- 3 large eggs
- ¼ cup granulated sugar
- 3 large egg whites
- A pinch of salt

For the Coffee Buttercream:
- 1 cup unsalted butter, at room temperature
- 2 tablespoons strong brewed coffee or espresso
- 1 ½ cups powdered sugar

For the Chocolate Ganache:
- ¾ cup heavy cream
- 6 ounces dark chocolate, finely chopped

For the Chocolate Glaze:
- 4 ounces dark chocolate, finely chopped
- ½ cup heavy cream
- 2 tablespoons unsalted butter

Directions

1. Preheat your oven to 375 F. Grease and line a baking sheet with parchment paper.
2. For the Joconde Sponge: In a large mixing bowl, whisk together the almond flour and powdered sugar. Add the whole eggs and mix until well combined.
3. In a separate bowl, whip the egg whites with granulated sugar and salt until stiff peaks form. Gently fold the whipped egg whites into the almond mixture. Finally, fold in the all-purpose flour.
4. Spread the batter evenly on the prepared baking sheet and bake for about 10-12 minutes or until the sponge is lightly browned and springs back when touched. Let it cool.
5. For the Coffee Buttercream: In a mixing bowl, beat the softened butter until creamy. Gradually add the powdered sugar and coffee and continue beating until the buttercream is smooth and fluffy.
6. For the Chocolate Ganache: Place the chopped chocolate in a heatproof bowl. In a small saucepan, heat the heavy cream until it just starts to simmer. Pour the hot cream over the chocolate and let it sit for a minute. Stir until the chocolate is completely melted and the ganache is smooth.
7. For the Chocolate Glaze: Heat the heavy cream in a small saucepan until it starts to simmer. Remove from heat and add the chopped chocolate and butter. Stir until the glaze is smooth and shiny.
8. To assemble the Opera Cake: Cut the cooled Joconde sponge into three equal-sized rectangular pieces. Place one piece on a serving platter. Spread half of the coffee buttercream over it, followed by a layer of chocolate ganache. Repeat with the second layer of Joconde, buttercream, and ganache. Top with the third layer of Joconde.
9. Pour the chocolate glaze over the top layer of the cake, spreading it evenly with a spatula.
10. Refrigerate the cake for at least 2 hours to set

Chocolate Brownies From 1895

Prep: 15 minutes – Cook: 45 minutes – Servings: 12
Calories: 240 – Fat: 12g – Carbs: 26g – Fiber: 2g – Sugar: 16g – Protein: 4g

The brownies from 1895 were likely a delightful treat of their time, but they would likely differ in flavor and texture from the brownies we cherish today. These brownies have a dense and chewy texture with a rich, fudgy center. They are made by using more chocolate or cocoa powder and less flour, resulting in an intensely chocolaty treat. These brownies feature a mix of chocolate and vanilla or cream cheese batter, swirled together to create a visually appealing marbled effect.

Ingredients

- ½ cup all-purpose flour
- 1 cup granulated sugar
- ½ cup (1 stick) unsalted butter
- 2 large eggs
- ½ cup chopped nuts (such as walnuts or pecans) - optional
- 1 teaspoon vanilla extract
- ½ cup cocoa powder
- A pinch of salt

Directions

1. Preheat the oven to 350 F. Grease and flour an 8-inch square baking pan.
2. In a saucepan, melt the butter over low heat. Once melted, remove the pan from heat and stir in the granulated sugar until well combined.
3. Beat the eggs in a separate bowl, then add them to the butter-sugar mixture, stirring until smooth.
4. Sift the flour and cocoa powder together, then gradually add them to the wet ingredients, stirring until just combined.
5. If using, stir in the chopped nuts and vanilla extract, and add a pinch of salt to enhance the chocolate flavor.
6. Pour the batter into the prepared baking pan, spreading it evenly.
7. Bake the brownies in the preheated oven for about 20-25 minutes or until a toothpick inserted into the center comes out with moist crumbs, but not wet batter.
8. Once done, remove the brownies from the oven and allow them to cool in the pan before cutting them into squares and serving.

Angel Food Cake From 1900

Prep: 20 minutes – Cook: 1 hour & 20 minutes – Servings: 12
Calories: 160 – Fat: 1g – Carbs: 40g – Fiber: 1g – Sugar: 26g – Protein: 4g

Angel Food Cake is traditionally served plain or with a dusting of powdered sugar. It's a delightful and airy cake, perfect for summer days or as a light dessert option. Serve Angel Food Cake with fresh berries like strawberries, raspberries, blueberries, or a mixed berry compote for a burst of fruity sweetness. Add a tangy twist by drizzling the cake with a glaze made from lemon or orange juice mixed with powdered sugar.

Ingredients

- 1 cup cake flour
- 12 large egg whites, at room temperature
- 1 teaspoon cream of tartar
- 1 ½ cups granulated sugar
- 1 teaspoon vanilla extract
- ¼ teaspoon salt
- Optional: ½ teaspoon almond extract

Directions

1. Preheat your oven to 350 F.
2. Sift the cake flour and 3/4 cup of sugar together three times to ensure they are well combined and aerated.
3. In a mixing bowl, beat egg whites on low speed until frothy.
4. Add the cream of tartar and salt to the egg whites and continue beating on medium speed until soft peaks form.
5. Gradually add the remaining 3/4 cup of sugar to the egg whites, a little at a time, while continuing to beat the mixture. Beat until stiff peaks form, and the egg whites are glossy and smooth.
6. Gently fold in the vanilla extract and almond extract (if using).
7. Gradually sift and fold the dry ingredients (cake flour and sugar mixture) into the egg whites, about 1/4 cup at a time, until fully incorporated.
8. Carefully transfer the batter into an ungreased tube pan (angel food cake pan).
9. Bake in the preheated oven for about 35-40 minutes or until the top is golden brown and the cake springs back when lightly touched.

10. Remove the cake from the oven and immediately invert the pan onto a wire rack to cool completely. This helps prevent the cake from collapsing as it cools.
11. Once the cake is completely cool, run a knife around the edges of the pan to release the cake.

Sign-up Now
and Be Notified of New Books

Website: readbooks.today

Made in the USA
Las Vegas, NV
26 December 2024

15423939R00059